GET IT

The Go Getter's Playbook

GET IT

The Go Getter's Playbook

A Ron's Life Speaks Experience

Ron Elliott Jr.

GET IT
The Go Getter's Playbook

Published by Invisible Clouds, LLC
Written by Ron Elliott Jr.

ISBN-13: 978-0-692-74788-9

Printed in the United States of America

I dedicate this book to everyone working hard to discover themselves. This is for every dreamer, builder, doer; for all of the "Davids" committed to slaying the giants in their lives.

Help a young person get started on the right path!
Visit Huddleupkids.com to Learn How

Losing Ain't an Option (We Winning)

Losing ain't an Option
I want the top spot in the top ten
so I run more, I run harder
I study the game, I run smarter
I'm up early, I'm on the field
I'm up late, I'm watching film
Look at these moves I'm making,
Look at these fools I'm shaking
I paid my dues no faking
no counterfeits my count's legit
I'm putting up them numbers
and numbers don't lie
I play to win refuse to lose, I know the rules don't break them
challenges I take them
snap them no snap backs
Detroit fitted my backpack
got my playbook, I'm a Go Getter
On the mound I'm a perfect pitch
call me Mr. No Hitter
I'm no quitter, a Gorilla, there's no realer competitor
if I fall I get up don't know what it is to give up
I get stronger, faster, train even longer
pass the test, past the rest
Cause I put that work in
Look how hard I workout
I deserve to be all I am
I deserve to be champion
Somebody loses every game
I can't be them
Can't be them

Acknowledgements

First and foremost, I must give all praise to my Lord and Savior, Yeshua the Messiah. Before experiencing the grace of YHWH, I lived a life destitute of purpose and filled with destruction. If not for the light of the Messiah, I would truly be dead. Now I live a life full of purpose and love. To my wife Mari, thank you for loving me. To Samia, Aniya, Alaina, and Sophia, everything I do, I do for you. You are my inspiration to be a better person, a better son, a better husband, and a better father. I want to thank my mother for loving me and raising me to be my own person. I want to thank my Aunt Benita and Uncle Val for always believing in my dreams and encouraging me to attain them. To my closest friends that hold me accountable to my purpose—AT, Carlton, B-Money, Cochise, Johnny Mack, Dub (RIP) and Mike G—you brothers help me to stay on track when I want to go on a tangent and explore all of my awesome ideas at one time. Thank you for the reality checks, the prayers, and words of encouragement in regards to pursuing my purpose without fear. The conversations we have had about this process have really helped me do what it takes to change millions of lives.

Damien (Cochise), I want to especially thank you for opening my mind to the possibilities of just being myself and that being enough to be great. To my contemporaries working to change the world one word at a time... Arvell, DeAndre Carter, Brian Maxwell, Monica Marie Jones, and J McGhee, keep grinding; you are making a difference. To one of my mentors and inspiration to pursue my dreams boldly, Mr. Hajj Flemings, thank you for all of the jewels and for leading by example. S/O to D. Reed and Kim Brooks for always being willing to share openly about the craft.

Special thanks to my Yunion family for the opportunity to share my gifts and talents with the audience that needs it most. Your effort, hard work, and dedication to families and youth will definitely receive an eternal reward. To all of my family and friends that I may not have mentioned, I love you! Lastly, shout to Dr. Eric Thomas who let me know that I can wear my Detroit-fitted jeans, and tee and still have a global impact. God bless you all!

Contents

Preface 1

Introduction 4

A Bentley Called Desire Play # 1 – Be Genuine 12

The Executioner's Execution Play # 2 – Execute 44

Tee It Up Play # 3 – Tact 66

Central Intelligence Agency Play # 4 – Be Intelligent 87

Time After Time Play # 5 – Value Time 122

Preface

When I received the call to begin speaking to youth professionally, it was a moment of confirmation for me. I had recently started a tech company and realized I didn't like it. I'd made up my mind that I wanted to speak, but I did not know my demographic. Who was my audience? There were many doubts and reasons for why I wasn't good enough or why I wouldn't fit in. In my mind, motivational speakers were rich and wore suits. I was far from rich and I was so Hip Hop, as a result of being a professional musician for so long that I couldn't get into the suit thing. It wasn't until my friend, and fellow author Damien "Cochise Tarak Saa" McSwine, encouraged me to check out ET the Hip Hop Preacher. He said, "Ron, it's a guy from your hood, dressed just like you, and killing YouTube—doing exactly what you want to do!" ET and his Detroit fitted were awesome and exactly what I needed to see.

At first I felt defeated, like I was beaten to the punch. But after doing some research and really digging into ET, I realized that I had a different story and approach. I was inspired and encouraged by his energy and rawness. I was ready to take it to the next level.

Then I got a call from a friend asking me if I'd be willing to work with youth. The obvious answer was "yes". I was very nervous, to be honest. I wasn't nervous about speaking, I'd done Toastmasters for a month or so and according to a few great speakers in my club, I was a natural and really did not need them. Despite the praise, I wasn't sure about working with youth. I did it and had a huge impact on a hundreds of youth. I've executed over 200 workshops and had the pleasure to learn a lot from my co-laborers that were more experienced. I grew in my confidence to provide high quality content to a variety of people, very quickly.

I wrote this book to share all of the stored up knowledge that I have acquired through life experiences and observation. Pastor Johnson (RIH), a mentor, once told me, "We are like funnels for God. The blessing isn't for us to hold onto. It is poured into us with the intention to fill up His people and as a result, we are first to taste the blessing." This book is a funnel. I've learned so much from the insights and stories. Writing this helped to confirm my purpose. In it you will learn:

- How to discover your purpose and be genuine
- How to execute your plan
- How to strategically leverage your relationships
- How to leverage your knowledge and personal intelligence
- And you will learn to value your time

The five steps mentioned in this book can be applied to helping you become a person worthy of having everything you want in life. This work is intended to help you fulfil the God given purpose placed on your life and live happily and joyously while having a positive impact on the world. It is my hope that you will be empowered and charged to: **Build a Home. Teach a Class. Start a Revolution.**

It is not about what you "Get." It is about who you inspire.
–Ron

Introduction

It was a black limousine. A gentleman stepped out through the rear doors lavishly dressed in a black tuxedo. I was watching TV with my grandmother, sitting on the floor in the living room and picking at my grandmother's feet (eew), when I saw the driver open the door for this most distinguished gentleman. I said, "I want one of those." My grandmother said, "Those cars are for rich people." At that point, I knew I wanted to be rich. I was six years old when I made this declaration. I wasn't sure what "rich" was but I knew we were not "it," and I wanted "it."

Robin Leach and the *Lifestyles of the Rich and Famous* excited me. I wanted a life of luxury but had no clue or idea of how to attain it. There were not many visible options on Euclid and Wildemere or Ohio and Joy Rd., in Detroit. The most successful people that I witnessed in real life sold drugs. The closest thing to a startup was a crack house down the street. And though I did not have many examples of "success," I had a hustler's ambition boiling in my bloodstream. I discovered later in life that my dad's mom was a numbers lady for the mob and bootlegged moonshine.

Made sense. Always seemed like my granny had cash stashed somewhere when you really needed it. My mom's dad, with only a third grade education, owned a restaurant. He was a proud man. He worked for himself doing what he loved but it was really just a job. It never took him to the promise land. I inherited my entrepreneurial spirit from my grandparents. My first business was selling cookies and candy at granddaddy's restaurant. These two people were my superheroes growing up. They were the kindest, most giving people I'd ever known. (Plus the best cooks!) So it made sense to me to challenge my mom's programming of, "Go to school, get a good job, and live the American Dream."

I was born a Go Getter. I wasn't aware of any gifts or talents growing up, but I always wanted more. I developed a relentless work ethic in everything I did. My first conquest was football. That didn't work out too well. Lasted maybe a month. I remember my mom and stepfather grilling me about quitting and not letting me do anything else. I begged and begged to play basketball. I do not remember who caved first (in retrospect, I think it was my stepfather), but they let me try out for the team. Basketball became my everything. I developed into a great player. Injuries and the wrong school choice eliminated my chances of playing professionally so I decided in 11th grade that I was going to be an entrepreneur.

I began in the music business. I started in artist management, then became an artist, producer, and eventually the owner of my own label and publishing company. I learned early that being an entrepreneur meant no sleep, no help, and a lot of learning. After years of being a professional musician, I became dissatisfied with the direction of the business. There had to be something just as fulfilling as the art but without the watered down messages and lack of creativity.

Creating and being on stage are by far two things that I absolutely love doing. Making music was fun but the pressure to conform for success was too much. I could not sell out. That also meant, I could not get paid so I had to make music a hobby. But I still wanted that thrill, I still wanted to help people change their lives and I wanted to be able to feed my family doing what I loved. The only thing I could think of that would allow me to have an impact and continue to do what I love was speaking. I could create, impact lives positively, be on stage, and make money!

My perception of a great motivational speaker was someone that was wealthy and taught people how to amass great wealth. With that thought, I created a roadblock for myself. I was not wealthy therefore I was not qualified. I made up my mind that I would do something to make a lot a money and then talk about that. This was my first mistake.

I started by chasing the money instead of purpose. In 2012-2013, technology was a big deal in Detroit. I wanted the fastest track to success. I learned how to do websites over the years and had a few ideas for an app. I created the app and began marketing it. I learned quickly that I was ahead of the curve. The market for my app was not ready for such technology. Therefore, I began to focus more on web development. Business was good but I was miserable. I did not like doing the work. I was able to create, that was fun, but the endless tweaks and back and forth changes with clients was driving me crazy. I was not living the life I'd imagined.

Simultaneously while running my tech startup, I was dabbling in the fitness arena. I'd just lost 25 pounds and was inspiring quite a few people with my transformation. I began getting requests to train people. I thought it would be a fun thing to do on the side, so I became a certified trainer and group fitness instructor. The more my distaste for the tech business increased, the more time and energy I spent with my new fitness business. To add another layer to my complex life, I took a contract to facilitate workshops in metro area schools. From the outside looking in, I was pretty successful. I was getting paid to do what I loved to do. I must admit for a time it was cool. My fitness business was growing, I was slowly working my way out of the tech business and I was getting a lot of speaking engagements. But I wasn't getting rich. In fact, I was just getting by. What was I doing wrong?

Just as I began to build momentum for my fitness business, my wife and I found out we were expecting. What we were not expecting was twins. The bigger her belly became, the more problems we had. She eventually had to go on bed rest and that ruined my business. Her being on bed rest required me to be home to take care of our nine and five-year-old girls in the evenings. I had to let go of training and classes in the evenings.

Knowing I had two kids and two more on the way put a lot of pressure on me to replace my lost income. I was still speaking, but I picked up a part-time job for a couple hours during the day and began a home-based internet business to make up for my lost income. I went from growing to fighting to survive. I lost sight of what I really wanted to do and started doing whatever I could to take care of my family. I began taking every income opportunity that came my way. At one point, I was operating five businesses at one time just to pay the bills. I was stretching myself way too thin. Some of my friends with lesser resolve thought I was a superhero for doing so much. I just wanted to do one thing, but I did not value my experiences, I wasn't confident enough in my gift, and I was afraid to risk it all to pursue my passion. You have to be willing to Risk It All!

The turning point came when I made up my mind to just do it. I had a few key conversations with business partners and friends that confirmed that I just needed to go for it. So I did. And guess what, it worked! I am not "rich" yet by financial standards, but I am wealthy. I am finally doing what I love and having a huge impact in my community. I have now delivered over 200 workshops helping people develop their character. I am living my purpose. I am able to be on stage, use my gifts, and impact lives without compromising my identity.

Personal Achievement is an admirable desire. Recently, I've taken a psychological assessment. It identified my number one desire as helping people. A close second was making money. Finally, it stated that I like fame. The results were accurate. Helping people "become" is the leading motivational factor for everything I do. Money is important, the more I have the more people I can help. Fame is a necessary evil. I am ok with being in the background. I do however love the stage. The energy of thousands of people in a room going nuts is unbelievable. It charges my battery to see people excited about growing.

In addition to my psychological assessment, I also took a personality test. I learned that only 3% of people are like me in the world. People with my personality type are leaders, politicians, CEOs, entrepreneurs, or philosophers. I am strategic, efficient, charismatic, and have a "no quit," get-it-done type of persistence. (Didn't need a test for this but it confirmed some things.)

I'm a man of faith. I believe, unashamedly, in seeking purpose through YHWH. To sum up my personal self-assessment, I took a spiritual gifts test as well. The test was further confirmation for the path I have chosen. I possess the spiritual gifts of wisdom, faith, and encouragement. I provide these types of assessments in my workshops to help participants get on the right path to success. You must know thyself!

The title of this book tells you there are five steps to getting everything you want out of life. This is the small print. You can get whatever you want out of life if you want what is right for you. A mind boggling concept, right? Many gurus sell you the dream that you can have all of the money, all of the influence, and every dream come true. Sounds great in theory, but the desired outcome doesn't always materialize. Having all of the money and being a dope fiend will end your life prematurely, right? The purpose of this book is to guide you in really getting everything that is meant for you. If you are 4 foot 11, 20 years old, and have no athletic ability... the chances of you becoming an NBA superstar are below zero. I do not care how many times you tell yourself that you will achieve it... or how hard you work... that's a wrap. However, you may have a gift for math and create a startup that makes you so rich that you can own an NBA team!

In this book you will learn how to want the right things and how to become the person worthy of attaining those desires. To become "worthy", you have to know your purpose, you have to execute, you must leverage relationships and your intelligence, and you must value your time. These steps will help you "become."

Everyone wants to be successful! I encourage you to look beyond success. Success is a selfish pursuit. Success is vain because we seek to achieve it mostly for personal satisfaction. I believe Jay Z said it best, "What do I think of success? It sucks, too much stress..."

My hope is that after reading this book, you will shift your mindset from success to significance. It doesn't take much more than caring to be significant. Significance is driven by a desire to add value to the world. Remember your favorite teacher? What about the things you learned from your coach? If you grew up in the "hood," you may have picked up a few lessons from an OG that helped you escape the trap. Significance! You may never become rich and famous, but you have the potential to impact the many lives you come into contact with on a daily basis. I am not suggesting to you to throw away your goals or desires to achieve success. I am suggesting that you open your eyes to the bigger picture. Success alone is hardly remembered and easily disappears. Success comes and goes. Success does not create a fulfilling life. Mike Tyson was a successful boxer... but a poor businessman. Michael Jordan was a successful basketball player but failed at being a husband. Success is great while it lasts, but significance is great because it lasts. I want you to be the greatest "you" that you can be.

Have you ever set a goal and failed to achieve it? Maybe you wanted to get an A+ on a test. Or, you tried to lose weight and it never seemed like you could drop those pounds, no matter how hard you tried. What if I told you I know the secret to succeeding at all the things you want to do? Assuming money is a non-factor, what would you be willing to pay to discover the secret that eludes 90% of people? Would you be willing to spend time examining your life, thoughts, and desires? Would you be willing to write these things down? Would you be willing to do whatever it takes to get them?

GET IT is the Go Getter's Playbook. A Go Getter is someone that does not sit around waiting for things to happen, but someone that makes things happen. You are the Playmaker and I am your personal Phil Jackson, a Zen Master, designing the Triangle Offense for your life. Every *Champion* has a great *Coach* to help guide them in the right direction. I cannot live your life for you. I can, however, share with you the wisdom I have acquired through experience and careful study from other great teachers.

This playbook is designed to be a straight to the point guide to getting you on the fast track to success, and from success to significance. I want to see you win. Let's GET IT!

A Bentley Called Desire
Play # 1 – Be Genuine

"To build a fast car, a good car, the best in its class."
- W.O. Bentley

When W.O. Bentley created the first Bentley, it was more of a race car than a luxury vehicle. Bentley's name is revered today, but Mr. Bentley himself had little to do with it. After losing his company, he went on to work for Rolls Royce and Aston Martin. Bentley's desire was never the riches. He was more of a tinkerer, an engineer by trade. And despite three failed marriages and being forced out of his own company, he held true to his genuine desire to build fast cars, good cars, and best-in-class cars.

To be a Go Getter, one must be genuine. You must have a genuine desire, a genuine faith, and a genuine purpose if you want to leave a significant mark in this world.

"SAY IT FROM THE BOTTOM"

You have to be living under a rock if you haven't heard of Eric Thomas, aka ET the Hip Hop Preacher. ET is a motivational powerhouse. A Detroit native, who at one point was homeless, he's now one of the most in demand speakers of today. His rise to success can be traced to a pivotal moment in YouTube history, when a story he shared with a group of students at Michigan State University became a viral hit.

Here is the story:

A young man desires to become a successful millionaire, so he goes to see the wise guru, who knows the ultimate secret to success. The young man says to the teacher, "I want to become rich and successful. Can you help me?" The guru smiles and says, "Meet me at the beach tomorrow at 4 AM, and I will tell you the secret to success."

So the next morning, the young man shows up on the beach at 4 AM, just like the guru had asked, wearing a suit and tie. Upon arriving, he realizes that the guru is already in the water swimming, dressed not in a suit and tie, but in a pair of swimming trunks. The guru spots the young man and motions for him to come in the water. So the young man goes knee-deep into the water. "Come out further," the guru says. "This is an expensive suit," the young man replies, "I came here to learn the secret to success, not the secret to swimming."

"The secret must be told in this water. It is your choice to learn the secret or not." So the young man goes waist-deep into the water, soaking his expensive suit. "Farther," the guru says. The young man becomes irritated. "Listen old man," he says with impatience, "I'm already in the water. I didn't come here for a swimming lesson. Tell me the secret to success right now or I'm leaving."

The guru, unaffected by the young man's outburst, replies calmly, "You are already waist-deep. What's a few more steps?" So the young man wades deeper into the water until the water is up to his neck. The sun is beginning to rise. "So tell me the secret," the young man demands. The guru says, "Sure," and suddenly forces the young man's head under the water. The young man, caught off guard, swallows salty sea water by accident and begins to drown. He flails his arms and tries to push the guru off him, but the guru continues to hold the young man's head underwater, using all of his strength to keep him there.

Just before the young man loses consciousness, the guru pulls the young man back up, who begins coughing immediately and gasping for air. The guru immediately asks the young man a question: "When your head was under water, what did you want to do?" "Kill…you…" the young man sputtered out between hacking coughs. He grabs onto the guru with the intention of drowning him, but the young man is still trying to recover and is unable to push the guru's head underwater.

"Besides that," the guru said, pushing the young man's hands off him. The young man coughs some more. He looks up at the guru and sees that he is still looking at him, waiting for a response. His stern look causes the young man to become enraged. "I WANTED TO BREATHE!"

He shoves the guru aside violently and begins stumbling towards the shore, coughing up seawater as he wades and splashes. What the guru says next however, stops the young man in his tracks: "When you want success as much you wanted to breathe just now when you were drowning, then, and ONLY THEN, will you have success." And with that, the guru goes back to swimming.

"When you want to succeed as bad as you want to breathe, then you will succeed..." has become a common mantra among young people worldwide that want to "Get It." At the root of this statement is **Desire**.

Desire, by definition is to want or wish for something. The desire it takes to be a Go Getter exceeds a simple wish. The desire to achieve all that you want is one that is a burning flame inside of your soul.

THE WILL TO WIN

Michael Jordan was my childhood hero. I will take this moment to apologize in advance if I reference MJ more than once in my writing. I'm sorry, I used to "wanna be like Mike." In context to desire, MJ was the poster boy. We all have heard the story of Michael Jeffrey Jordan overcoming being cut from his high school team, to becoming the greatest basketball player ever. Winning six championships definitely speaks to his will to win. In 1997, I was a freshman in college, home for the summer working at Papa Romano's Pizza. During the playoffs, the owner would take myself and a few friends to the nearest sports bar to watch the playoff games. I remember it like it was yesterday. Everyone with me hated "Da Bulls," and I was the lonesome Jordan fan. It was Game 5 of the NBA playoffs, or as history refers to it: the "Flu Game."

Legend has it that MJ called his trainer to his hotel room, where he was lying in the fetal position and sweating profusely. He hardly had the strength to sit up in bed and was diagnosed with a stomach virus or food poisoning, likely caused by a pizza ordered the night before. The Bulls' trainers told Jordan that there was no way he could play the next day. Momentum was on the side of the Utah Jazz who had just won Games 3 & 4 of the championship series. Jordan stayed in the bed the entire day. Then about an hour before tip-off, heads to the game.

Watching on television, it was obvious that Mike was not himself; you could see it in his eyes. He looked a step slower than usual and of course the announcers let us know that he had "flu like symptoms." The first quarter belonged to the Jazz. The second quarter, MJ had arrived. I remember the announcer saying something like, "Not bad for a guy playing with flu symptoms." By halftime the Bulls only trailed by four points. Now if you asked the other team, they'd say Jordan was faking. However, it would diminish the legend of the event to accept that theory, so for the sake of the story we are going to stick with the "flu like symptoms" theory. In the end, the Bulls won and MJ scored 38 points to carry his team to victory. Despite his physical ailment, Jordan willed his team to victory. Michael loved to win and strongly desired another championship. This game is a great example of leaving it all on the court to get the victory.

Another great story about the desire to win can be traced back to the story of Alexander the Great. As the story goes, Alexander and his troops were outnumbered when they arrived on the shore of Persia for war. Legend has it that he told his army to burn their ships. The burning of the ships meant there was no way to retreat, making the genuine desire to win a desire to live rather than die.

"We go home in Persian ships or we die."
-Alexander the Great

YOUR FAITH HAS MADE YOU WELL

Luke 8:42-48:

As Jesus went, the people pressed around him. **43** And there was a woman who had had a discharge of blood for twelve years, and though she had spent all her living on physicians, she could not be healed by anyone. **44** She came up behind him and touched the fringe of his garment, and immediately her discharge of blood ceased. **45** And Jesus said, "Who was it that touched me?" When all denied it, Peter said, "Master, the crowds surround you and are pressing in on you!" **46** But Jesus said, "Someone touched me, for I perceive that power has gone out from me." **47** And when the woman saw that she was not hidden, she came trembling, and falling down before him declared in the presence of all the people why she had touched him, and how she had been immediately healed. **48** And he said to her, "Daughter, your faith has made you well; go in peace."

Desire alone is not enough to acquire the things you want. There are many people that want to become rich, but so many are still poor. A cornerstone to the success puzzle is faith. One cannot achieve greatness if they lack the ability to believe. In the previous passage, we see a woman that is ill become healed by simply touching Jesus' garment. Now this isn't about whether you believe in Jesus or not, but for the sake of the story, the woman believed that there was healing in him. As a result, her faith, her strong unwavering belief that Jesus could heal her, healed her. Now if this woman stood in the crowd and said, "Jesus cannot heal me..." would she have been healed? Nope!

DON'T BELIEVE ME JUST WATCH

Have you ever learned to ride a bike? When you first started, you may have said, "I can't." And when you said, "I can't," you couldn't. As you began to pedal and your mom or dad held your seat, you began to grow in confidence. You began to believe, and at some point they let you go and you didn't fall because you developed the faith you needed, the trust you needed in yourself to succeed.

Faith and desire are a powerful tandem. Whether it is flying or visiting outer space, without a desire and without faith, nothing will happen. In some occasions this power coupling is not enough. In most cases without purpose, both faith and desire become orphans wandering in the universe without a home.

THE HOLY TRINITY- Desire, Faith, Purpose

"Gifts are given. Skills & talents are developed."
- Coach Ron

One thing that has always worked for me in any relationship has been my transparency. I am a big fan of a gentleman by the name of Jim Rohn. I recall listening to Mr. Rohn and him saying something to the effect of: "People do not want to hear from the person that fails, despite the fact that they can learn more about how to succeed by learning from their mistakes." I'm going to keep it one hundred with you, I've fallen time and time again. I didn't fall because I lacked faith or because I didn't have the desire to succeed. I have failed mostly because of lack of purpose.

As long as I can remember, I have always had to work my butt off to succeed. When I was 10 years old, I quit the football team to play basketball because I really did not enjoy the hits I was taking being on the A team instead of the D team where I belonged. I was pretty tall for my age. Unfortunately, I stopped growing at 14.

My ten-year-old self sucked at hooping. Our uniforms had those "brief" looking shorts. My socks with red and blue stripes were up to my knees, I wore huge red knee pads, and sported a pair of those clunky goggles. It was a bad look. I used to think my coaches let me play because they felt sorry for me. I later learned they let me play because despite not being the most talented player, I played hard. I scrapped for every rebound and dove for every loose ball. And like most young guys, I started taking notice that the guys that got the most love were those that scored the most points. I had the fire then at the tender age of ten to become the best. I wanted to win.

In the summer I would play with the older guys every day. I would practice jumping every day. I would practice shooting every day. Every day over the course of the next three years I watched Michael Jordan, studied his moves and lived basketball. Needless to say, by the time I was 13 I was a heralded and accomplished player. My team was one of the best 8th grade teams ever assembled. I played with some of the best AAU talent in the state. If you asked me at that time in my life, I was sure that I would make it to the NBA. I mean I was dunking the ball in 8th grade, averaging 20 points and 15 rebounds a game. I surely was going to the league.

Every high school wanted me. But my mother had her sights set on one in particular. My coach told me to go to a school called Renaissance

High in Detroit. It was a public school that was big on academics but lacked severely in athletics. He had a great relationship over there and knew that I could start on varsity as a freshman. This is the path to greatness in the world of basketball. However, my mother was wooed by the coach of Cass Tech. He came to our home, was very personable and ensured my mother that it was the best place for me to be. So guess what, I went to Cass.

Cass was a great school. It was very big. It also had a lot of talent and competition. When I arrived at Cass, there were a few people there that I played AAU ball with; great players. The problem with Cass was that the coaches did a great job of recruiting and we were overrun with talent. And despite being recruited to be there, everyone still had to try out for the team.

IT WAS THE MOMENT I FEARED

One day, preparing for tryouts during a scrimmage at my old school, I pulled up for a three point shot. As I came down, I landed on the defender's foot, tearing the ligaments in my left ankle. It was an excruciating pain. I was so disappointed because at that point, I knew my season was over. After the injury, it seemed like the coach didn't know me anymore. It was like I was of no use to the team. He set me up on a church team when I was well enough to play again. Eventually, I made my way back on the team.

THE SOPHOMORE SLUMP

Sophomore year was even tougher than freshman year. Sophomore year was great in that we won the first ever JV championship.

However, it was all bittersweet because we had so many people on the team, and the JV coach despised me after my mother decided to confront him about my playing time. SMH… that was a bad move mom. Lol.

After my second year of high school, I took it up a notch. I worked with a personal trainer. I worked on all of my skills relentlessly. Funny enough, it seemed like the varsity coach took notice. During our summer league games, I ran the show. I was certain that I would get my shot. I did not. I mean, when I played outside of school in other leagues and pickup games, I bested those that were playing ahead of me. But inside of the system, I was always put on the shelf. I begged my mother to let me transfer. I figured if I made a move soon enough, I would have enough time to salvage my career. My mother wasn't trying to hear it. "Work harder she said…" at that point basketball became more of a minimum wage job than a career in something I enjoyed, so I quit. Most people will tell you, "Don't quit; don't give up."

The truth is, when you have an investor's mind, you don't fall in love with one stock. You create your basket and you ride with the winners. When a stock is up and not profiting, sell, sell, sell! There was no more upside in basketball for me. It was time to move on.

YOU GOTTA LOVE IT, BABY BABY!

After quitting the basketball team, I couldn't help but think about my future. For a great part of my life, basketball was my meal ticket. Basketball saved my life in that it gave me something to pursue other than the streets, which were so tempting to me as a youth. I remember walking down the hallway at school thinking, "What else do you love?" The only thing I could come up with was music. There was one problem standing in my way however: I couldn't sing, rap, or play any instruments. How in the world would I make money in the music business?

Honestly, I am not sure where I got the idea that if you are going to do something in life that you should love it. But at the age of 16, I was bent on finding a way to turn my love for music into cold hard cash. I grew up listening to great music all of my life. My biological father was a musician, ironically. I recall watching a Notorious B.I.G. video and paying very close attention to this guy dancing around in the video saying, "Yea, yea… take that…" In my mind at that point, I automatically associated Puff Daddy, or as you know him today, Sean P. Diddy Combs, as the money man. I started looking at every record to see what he contributed and studying the music business. I decided that I was going to be a producer because I knew what was hot and was willing to pay to get it done.

Again, in my mind I did not have any musical talent, gift, or skill. But one of my friends from school could rap and could rap well. I was so impressed with his ability to freestyle that I was ready to bet all of my money on his career. I worked a part-time job to save up enough money to put him in the studio. However, whenever it was time to work, the "Biggie" to my "Puffy" was nowhere to be found. After getting burned so many times, I decided to take matters into my own hands and started teaching myself how to rap. By the time I graduated high school, I knew what I wanted to do, and believed I could pull it off with the right amount of practice and time.

GROWING PAINS

At 17 years of age, I told my mother that I had a plan. It was a simple plan, and till this day I believe that if I followed it, my path would have been much easier. But Jay Z taught me in 1996 that, "You gotta learn to live with regrets." Besides, this book would not be as interesting if I skyrocketed to success, right?

My plan went as follows:

1. Get a job at the plant (Chrysler, Ford, GM).
2. Live at home, pay rent, stack my chips for five years.
3. Buy a home and start my record company.

I still think this was a great plan, but my mother was in no way going for this. One of her only dreams in life was for me to graduate from college. Her mindset was (she no longer thinks like this) that if you go to college, you will be able to get a good job and then you can do what you want. I, of course, didn't agree but I had too much respect for my mom to do anything other than honor her request. (Lesson: Follow your heart!)

My first year of college was fun, historical, and fretful. I remember being in my dorm room watching TV when they announced that 2Pac was shot. And I was in my apartment the next semester when I got a call from a friend to turn on the tube because Biggie was gunned down. I also remember school being hard, spending a lot of time writing rhymes, and almost getting kicked out for my lack of performance. I spent my entire second semester just trying to stay in school and not disappoint my mom.

Year two was when I started to catch my stride. I changed my major a few times until I found out that marketing was the most natural for me. I made the dean's list and spent all of my time doing a limited number of activities including: writing, rapping, recording, playing NBA Live, lifting weights, and basketball. I went to class almost never… If you are a student, I do not recommend this plan.

Year three, I began to get pretty good at rapping. I'd won some talent shows and performed at a few big venues. Things were good but it was hard to find beats. I quickly took matters into my own hands and bought my first studio equipment. I think I made at least 10 beats a day for the next year trying to figure out how Timbaland and Dr. Dre made those awesome beats.

In my senior year I spent most of my time driving to the city, working, hitting the studio, and driving back to school. I was doing a lot more shows, and I released my first official single. I was officially a business owner. I took a huge loss but I felt accomplished at the end of the day and I believed I had what it took to be great. I still feel I have what it takes and my catalogue is pretty dope (IJS).

Upon graduating, I took a job in Atlanta and began to expand on my skill set. I released my first group album with a friend and we became fairly popular on the scene. We had music playing in the clubs, were working our single on the radio and were one miscommunication away from a record deal with Bad Boy Records and TVT.

At this point in my life, I was super confident in my ability to succeed in this business. However, things took a turn for the worst with my health, and then my job, and finally my money. I'll save the "What

Happened" for another book. Just know like any champ, I got knocked down, got up, and KO'd the sucker that thought he was going to get my belt.

Obviously, I did not become a huge hip hop star. If you visit my website: antscant.com, you can download a free song. You'll see that I have the skills, but the truth is, I was limited by solely focusing on music. Music for me is a tool, not a calling. I was so close to my purpose with music but a slight shift of perception changed everything for me. Now music is a huge part of what I do, but it is not what defines who I am.

Purpose has everything to do with true success. Sometimes, no matter how good you are, or how hard you work, things out of your control will steer you in a different direction. When you have a clear understanding of your purpose, you will begin to see the bigger picture. When you see who you are supposed to be, you can begin to walk in your truth. When you walk in your truth you will begin to develop into the person that is worthy of all that life has to offer. The difference in being successful and purposeful is simple. Success (perception wise) has an end. Purpose is a process. As people, we are always in process. Desire, faith, and purpose must constantly be present for you to have the life you want and to be able to enjoy it.

DREAM BIG!

Christopher Wallace—The Notorious B.I.G., Biggie Smalls, The Black Frank White, self-proclaimed King of New York—went from being a Brooklyn crack dealer to becoming a rap god. A masterful storyteller with the ability to create movie like imagery with words,

Biggie Smalls was one of the most influential motivational rappers ever. Forget about all of the violence, sexism, etc. and keep in mind the rags to riches story.

Earlier in the chapter I referenced my friend that possessed a very similar gift as the late great MC. There was a huge difference in the two that explains why we are still singing "Biggie, Biggie, Biggie, can't you see…," and why you have never heard of my friend. This difference can be summarized by the concept of vision. I honestly do not believe my friend could see himself being as great as his potential predicted. And because of his lack of vision, his dream faded away into a distant memory. Biggie on the other hand DREAMED BIG… PUN intended (that was a double- entendre by the way). (If you didn't get it, don't worry, it's something master MC's master… and another one, uh!)

OK, back to dreaming BIG. On B.I.G.'s first album he made his hit-making presence known with the song "Juicy," which sampled Mtume's "Juicy Fruit." "Juicy" was a celebratory song that took us on the journey from "ashy to classy." In the first verse Biggie starts with:

It was all a dream
I used to read Word Up magazine
Salt-n-Pepa and Heavy D up in the limousine
Hanging pictures on my wall
Every Saturday Rap Attack Mr. Magic, Marley Marl…
Now I'm in the Limelight cause I rhyme tight

Notorious B.I.G. was teaching us in our language how to win. He dreamed. When he was reading those magazines and looking at the pictures, he saw himself. He was in love with the culture, with the art. His dedication to the art paid off big time. Unfortunately, his powerful words about death and his demise, like his contemporary 2Pac, ended his run much too early.

On his "Life After Death" album, he left us with these uplifting lyrics however:

Sky's the limit and you know that you keep on
Just keep on pressing on
Sky's the limit and you know that
You can have what you want, be what you want...

I personally believe that Biggie was meant to be a MC. It was so effortless for him. He had the gift, he developed the skills, and unfortunately, he had a vision. His vision was that of his demise. Here is an important lesson in being genuine... when you continuously think about something and speak about it, you will attract it. Be careful with "keeping it real." Know the power of your words and how they can influence your world.

> *"The person that says she can, and the person*
> *that says she cannot, are both correct."*
> *–Unknown*

PASSION PURSUES PURPOSE

I am not a betting man, but I bet you that there has not been a person born yet that entered this world with an instruction manual. That's a pretty safe bet! When a child is born, parents have so much joy or fear... and then the focus becomes caring and providing for the child. As the child grows very little time is spent on discovering the child's purpose. The child gets older, experiments with "this," tries "that," becomes an adult and settles for whatever crumbs life has given him. This is not the rule, more like the trend. Just think about how many people you know that are working jobs they hate, just to survive. It is most difficult to perform consistently at a high level doing something that you are not passionate about. And if you do have a job that you are not passionate about, it is likely that you make enough money to do the things you love in another capacity.

THE NEIGHBOR'S PIANO

Margaret and John grew up on the west side of Detroit. They had a friend named Stevie Judkins. They all shared a love for music. John and Stevie had their own group performing throughout the neighborhood. Stevie, was a very musical youth and when he showed interest in the piano, Margaret taught him how to play with both hands, instead of just two fingers. Stevie said one day to Margaret, "If I could beat you playing piano one day, that would be the best thing in the world." After getting a handle on the piano, it seemed as if Stevie didn't want to do anything but music.

John's cousin, Ronnie, was a singer with Motown Records. John introduced Stevie to Ronnie, and Ronnie, introduced Stevie to Berry Gordy, the founder of Motown. John and Stevie auditioned for Mr. Gordy and both young men received record deals. John was 13 and Stevie was only 11. Stevie Judkins became Little Stevie Wonder... and John went on to write a few hit songs after losing all of his wealth due to improper financial education.

Stevie Wonder is an example of passion pursuing purpose. I do not believe Stevie being blind was a coincidence in the larger scheme of things. When you listen to his music, it is so vivid, yet the pictures he paints are only inspired by his ears and the visions inside of his mind. Stevie Wonder did not let his lack of sight stop him from pursuing what he loved. Though he could not see with his eyes, he could see with his heart. Stevie Wonder's impact on the world through his music will last until the end of time. What visions do you see in your mind? Will you make them tangible? Will you make them real?

WHY???

I am a man of many experiences. I am so passionate about purpose because I have been searching for my purpose for a very long time. In my journeys I have always "tried" different things. As a very young boy, all I ever wanted was to be rich. Honestly, I did not know what rich was. I did not know that we were poor. However, I did know that there was something special about the people that rode in the back of limousines and I wanted to be one of those people. As my worldview continued to take shape, I began deciding what I wanted to do. I was not steered in a direction, I just started picking things that I thought would make me rich.

Basketball of course was the first of those things. I loved basketball. It was one of two things that I was truly passionate about. But I was only passionate about it because I thought it would make me MONEY! The second thing that I grew passionate about was music. I worked really hard at developing my craft. I still really enjoy music, but at the end of the day... I felt trapped and confined by the business of it. I still use music in my speaking business however because it is relevant to my story, it makes my presentation more unique.

During my brief stint as a network marketer (one of many experiences), I learned something that became invaluable to me. It was taught to me by Eric Worre. What I learned from Mr. Worre was this: You must have a strong "why" and money alone is not a strong enough reason to do anything. Now at this point in my life, I have a family, and my "why" is more than money; it is providing for my children, being with them, and raising them right. However, beyond my kids, I learned that I had to dig deeper than the surface reasons for what I chose to do with my life. In my time of reflection, I was reminded of a quote from the rapper Mos Def, now known by Yasiin Bey. The quote is from his joint collaboration with Talib Kweli, Blackstar. The album was one of my favorites while in college and from time to time... I find myself remembering a lot of the lyrics to songs even though I haven't listened to them in years... that is the power of auto-suggestion, but I'll get to that momentarily. The quote that put things in perspective was:

I'm trying to live right in the sight of God's Memory.
-Mos Def

Ask yourself this: What do I have to do to live right in the sight of God?

This question led me into some deep soul searching. It should lead you as well. This question should also lead you to a super strong "why." Additionally, I've added a few questions towards the end of this chapter to help you dig deep into discovering your "why." This is not a single day task. It will take reflection, meditation, prayer, and experimentation. Be patient with the process. Remember, we are always in process.

Scripture says in Psalms 37:4 (NLT), "Take delight in the LORD, and he will give you your heart's desires." Most people interpret this as God giving you what you want. Now there are many that delight in the Lord and never get anything they want... and I refuse to believe that God is a liar, so let's look at this from another angle. Putting all of the translation stuff aside... what if this is really saying, "Take delight in the Lord, and he will place desires in your heart."

Maybe it is saying he will give you the fuel for the fire. I am no expert, but I'd like to believe that living right in the sight of God would be to live fulfilling a purpose. A purpose that you naturally have a desire for, a genuine desire, should easily produce a strong "why." In the end, more than just taking care of my kids, I want to leave a legacy of empowering people to discover their purpose and live it with passion. My personal mission statement is: **Build a Home. Teach a Class. Start a Revolution.** My greater "why" is to please God, to use my gifts, talents, and experiences to encourage others to do the same... that is my desire. That is my purpose...

LUCKY BUT LOST- Minecraft

Minecraft is the modern world's virtual Lego set that skyrocketed to success and captured the minds of millions. To date, the game has generated more than $700 million dollars. Minecraft is Googled more than the Bible, Harry Potter, and Justin Bieber. Minecraft proved to be a gold mine for its creator Markus "Notch" Persson when he sold Minecraft to Microsoft for $2.5 billion in cash. Minecraft was Markus' baby. Markus became rich fairly quick. His company with only 30 employees did $230 million in sales in 2012. Markus was able to pocket $101 million for his intellectual property.

Soon after the success of Minecraft, Persson stepped down as head developer of his company, lost his father to suicide, got married and divorced within a year and felt the weight of the world on his shoulders to recreate the magic of Minecraft. Because Persson was the brand, he took the blame from the gaming community when things were not right in the Minecraft universe. Markus could not take the negativity evoked by his online personality so he decided to plan an exit strategy. That exit strategy made him an instant billionaire and Microsoft the owners of the most popular video game of all time.

After the sale of his company, Markus began to party and live idly. He started a new company that exists solely in name. No ambition, no desire to do anything but play games online. Imagine the impact Markus could have on the world if he knew his purpose. Imagine the lives he could change if he knew why he had the platform he acquired.

Take a moment to reflect on your strong desires, your strong why. Why do you want the things you want? Will they just satisfy you, or will they leave an impression on the world long after you are gone? Being Genuine cannot be taken for granted. If you are not sincere about a thing, it will be very difficult to commit to it. Here's the monkey wrench... sometimes you have to build the desire... REMEMBER (auto-suggestion)?

THE BEST CONVERSATIONS

Some of the best conversations that I have ever had were with myself. This may sound a little vain but it isn't. The world as we know it will beat you down. Your family will doubt you, your friends will tell you that your ideas are crazy, some people will not show up to your event, others will not buy your product and what will you have left if you subscribe to their beliefs? ABSOLUTELY NOTHING! My conversations with self are the moments when I say, "You can do this Ron!" The truth is, sometimes you have to encourage yourself.

Every morning while taking my two oldest children to school, I have them say a few confessions. I encourage you to add something like this to your daily routine:

I HAVE BIG FAITH
I CAN
BECAUSE I WILL

Our minds, spirits, and souls need nutrition just like our body. We have to be careful what we allow into our minds through our eyes and ears. We have to be cautious about the information we ingest, the fear we absorb, the stinking thinking we let creep into our temples. The best way to condition your subconscious mind is to feed it good, healthy, clean, organic thoughts and ideas. If you create a culture of positivity in your inner being, that is what will begin to manifest in your life. Your faith will grow as you profess it to grow. If you tell yourself you can, losing will not be an option for you. Let's be honest, most of us are not born with great confidence. We develop confidence as we become good at things or are recognized for things that we do well. The best confidence to develop is Self Confidence. Here is my self-confidence formula:

1. I am created in the image and the likeness of the Most High God.
2. I have BIG FAITH, I CAN, BECAUSE I WILL.
3. I think about good things, perfect things, lovely things, anything that is virtuous.
4. Favor goes before me and prospers my way.
5. I speak only things that are good and edifying to those that hear.
6. I know what I want and I possess the ability to GET IT.
7. I do things decently and in order.

You have to believe without a doubt in your heart that you are worth it. You develop this belief, this faith, the fuel for the fire, by talking to yourself and planting these seeds of positivity and love into your subconscious mind.

God MC

The one person of my generation that has mastered this concept and made it pay big dividends is Jay Z. Jigga exudes supreme confidence in everything he does. His first album, Reasonable Doubt (which happens to be one of my favorite rap albums ever), sets the tone for his bravado. First, he and his partners put up their own money to release his music. This was done after a few labels refused to rock with Roc-a-fella. This was the era of million dollar videos and ridiculous budgets. The album boasted production and features from some of the dopest artists and producers out at the time. Biggie, Mary J Blige,

DJ Premier, just to name a few of the heavy hitters featured on the album. If no one believed before his album dropped, they all were put on notice afterwards. On Dead Presidents part 1 he says, "All rhymers forget it like Alzheimer's…" This is a bold statement considering the competitive nature and extreme talent of this particular era in hip-hop. The next year, he questioned, "Who's the best MC, Biggie, Jay-Z or Nas?" And with Biggie and Tupac gone, Jay crowned himself king and spoke it into fruition.

Now I don't want you to get this confused with hocus pocus voodoo. There is a science to this. It is quite simple. If you say something enough or hear something enough, you will start to believe it. If you believe it deeply enough, you will begin to act on it. When Jay Z claimed to be the best, he began to take more measures to prove it. Opportunity showed up, and did not have to knock. Jay was at the door waiting. What are your words attracting towards you? What conversations are you having with yourself? Are you the best? Or are you stupid? Do you always win? Or do you always lose? What is your standard? What is your highest expectation of yourself? You will live up to your highest expectation. Jay believed he was the best and became the best.

My oldest daughter sometimes throws pity parties. She'll say something like, "I always mess things up." I'll reply, "Be careful what you say about yourself. You will have what you say." I share with you this same wisdom. Say what you want, mean it, then do something to get it. The only obstacle that you are facing is you. Get out of your own way. Put in the mental work, put in the spiritual work, and put in the physical work to become a work of art.

Your desire may not be to build a fast car, a good car, a best-in-class car... but if you are reading this book, you do have a desire to have a purposeful life; an awesome life, the best life that you can possibly have. And if you are going to GET IT... you have to want it as badly as you want to breathe. You have to believe that it is attainable and you have to know why you really want it. You have to feed your desire for it, build your faith, and be Genuine. You have an amazing story to tell, for it to be told, you must live your life, with purpose.

There's a story I share in my talks. It is a great illustration of "Purpose". You can see the video at: diamondfeet.com.

The story goes a little something like this:

A guy wanted to succeed so bad that he went looking everywhere he could to find diamonds. He looked East. Travelled South. Searched West. And Explored North to no avail. Eventually he kills himself because he could not find the illusive stones.
When the guy left on his journey, he sold everything, even his home. The new homeowner, while walking his land discovered a ton of diamonds right where he stood. The moral of the story is this: You do not need to look further than yourself to discover what will make you successful or significant.
This is the short version... watch the video! Diamondfeet.com

Discovering Purpose

Warren Buffett, the Oracle of Omaha, has long been someone that I have admired. Mr. Buffett learned early in life how to make money. Warren studied under someone he trusted and admired, Ben Graham.

And while Warren Buffett followed in Mr. Graham's footsteps, he trail-blazed his own path with his own philosophy. Mr. Buffett's philosophy has helped him to amass a wealth of almost $60 billion. Warren knew at a young age what he wanted to do. He always had a business savvy mind. He always knew he wanted to be wealthy. He witnessed his father deal in stocks and in business. He started doing business young and made profits. The blueprint was set. The foundation was already in place. Mr. Buffett took the foundation and added to it to get what he wanted. Discovering your purpose is your foundation. This portion of the book is dedicated to just that. We've already established the importance of being genuine, having a strong desire, and possessing BIG FAITH. We know that purpose pursues passion and that we must have a strong WHY. Now let's take a look at some questions that will help us along the path.

Questions, Questions, Questions...

Below is a list of 25 questions to help you discover your passion. Discovering your passion will lead you on the path of purpose. Usually, the things that set us on fire have something to do with the problem we were created to solve in the world. Ultimately as you travel this road, you will have to spend some time with the Creator to learn what direction to move in. You will learn that you have many skills and desires and it is hard to choose what is most important.

There is a story about a conversation Mr. Buffett had with one of his employees. The conversation was about career goals. Mr. Buffett advised his employee to write a list of his top 25 career priorities. Warren asked his employee to circle the top five. The employee confirmed with Mr. Buffett that he would start working immediately on his top five goals. Mr. Buffett asked, "What about the other 20 goals?" The employee replied, "Those are important too. I will work on them when I can because they are not as urgent, but I will still dedicate time to them. At this point Mr. Buffett corrects his employee, "No. Everything you did not circle avoid! Do not seek to achieve anything until you achieve your top five goals.

Here is a list of questions to ask yourself to assist you in finding your passion.

1. What do you enjoy doing the most? What makes you happy?
2. What makes you feel like a superhero?
3. What do people ask your advice for?
4. What comes easy for you? What gifts do you have?
5. What problem in the world do you wish you could fix?
6. Who inspires you? Why?
7. Who are your mentors? What do they see in you? Why did you choose them?
8. What do you do and lose track of time while doing it?
9. If you won $3 million and never had to work again, how would you spend your time?
10. What would you do if success was guaranteed?
11. If you could have or do anything, what would it be?
12. What do you argue about the most? What do you feel strongly about?
13. What do you love helping others do?
14. What type of books do you like to read? Magazines?
15. When was the last time you could not sleep because you were so excited about something?
16. If you had to do a job for free for a year, what would it be?

17. If your spirit was at the front row of your home going service, what would you want people to say about you?
18. How do you want the world to remember? What mark do you want to leave in society?
19. What do your friends or family say that you'd be great at doing?
20. What do you find yourself naturally wondering about? What makes your curious?
21. What type of things do you google?
22. What did you want to be when you were a kid?
23. If you could write a self-help book, what would be the title?
24. What's your dream job?
25. What career or business opportunities are in line with your core beliefs?

Determine Your "Why"

If you took the time to answer all 25 questions you should feel empowered and motivated to discover your purpose. I believe passion pursues purpose. In other words, your passion will lead you to your purpose. Discovering your purpose is discovering your "Why!" Why were you created? What were you created to do? I believe the world would be a better place if it was filled with people doing exactly what they were created to do. In fact, we cheat the world and future generations when we do not become what we are intended to become.

I know personally that I've dilly dallied around, trying "this," trying "that," and ignoring my purpose, or loosely working towards it. I've been distracted, discouraged, and confused. I've also been on target, but afraid to leap. These experiences are universal for everyone. Rarely does an individual come into the world just knowing what to do and when to do it. Yes, some people discover these things early in life and it is evident of those that do. But most individuals never discover their hidden gifts and passions or attempt to realize them. YOU, will discover your gifts, develop your talents, and fulfill your purpose. You will become all that you are to be. I believe that anyone reading this book will seek to become what they were created to be. Here are a few more questions to ask yourself to help you discover your "why."

1. What do you do for a living?
2. Why do you do what you do for a living?
3. How does your work make you feel? How does it make you a better person?
4. How does what you do make others feel? How does it make the world better?
5. What is your core belief about life? What will you fight nail and tooth to defend?
6. What makes you nervous or angry about the current state of the world?
7. What do you fear most about future generations?
8. What does a perfect world look like?
9. What are the 5 things you are most passionate about?
10. Does your career allow you to fulfill the things you've listed in question 9?

If you answered "no" to question 10 you have some decisions to make. When we are young we equate success and happiness to riches and ignore purpose. And though I am not an expert on the Bible, there are two scriptures that come to mind in this matter:

1 Timothy 6:17

Charge them that are rich in this world, that they not be high-minded, nor trust in uncertain riches, but in the living God, who giveth us richly all things to enjoy; (KJV)

Titus 3:8

This is a trustworthy saying, and I want you to stress these things, so that those who have trusted in God may be careful to devote themselves to doing what is good. These things are excellent and profitable for everyone. (NIV)

Iron Mike

One of the most notable athletes of my time is Mike Tyson. Growing up, there were three "Mikes" everyone celebrated, Mike Jackson, Mike Jordan, and Mike Tyson the undisputed heavyweight champion of the world. Mike Tyson made history by becoming the youngest champion to win all three titles by the age of 20. He was also the first to hold all three titles at the same time. Over the course of his boxing career Mike Tyson earned more than $300 million dollars. At one point, Iron Mike was the man. He had money, had women, and was living the life. However, it wasn't a godly life. It wasn't a purposeful life. Mike Tyson was careless with money (trusting in uncertain riches), convicted of rape (high-minded) because he believed at a point in time the world owed him something because he was the champ. Eventually, Mike Tyson went broke, developed a drug addiction, and sadly, lost a child. Mike Tyson had the world, but the world wasn't enough. Riches did not make him happy. Riches destroyed him.

Imagine if Mike Tyson had a revelation of purpose as a young man. Imagine a Mike Tyson with a father that did not abandon his family. Imagine a Mike Tyson whose mother did not die when he was 16 years old. Imagine if Mike Tyson knew to use his fame to do good. Imagine the impact he would have had on the world. The purpose of this book is to help the next generation of stars, influencers, and leaders have the wisdom needed to make the right decisions despite their circumstances. Our circumstances are not prisons. Circumstances are simply hurdles that are meant to be leaped. Leave your excuses at the door. It is your turn to be undisputed. It is your time to be a champion. In a perfect world you'd have nothing to overcome. But this world isn't perfect! You are being equipped to be great. Be Great!!!

Kurt Cobainin' It

There are dangers associated with Godlessness. Kurt Cobain is an American Idol of sorts. A Rock and Roll Hall of Fame Inductee, many people credit Cobain as a revolutionary for Rock music. Cobain was the lead singer/songwriter for the group Nirvana. Their song "Teen Spirit" was a huge hit and one of few Rock songs that I actually liked growing up. Nirvana has sold over 75 million albums worldwide. Massive success was not enough for Kurt however.

As a teen it is reported that Kurt became a devout Christian. Later he renounced Christianity. He is quoted as writing, "God is gay." And while it is not my purpose to promote religion, only to share the importance of living a righteous life before the Creator, I cannot help but to believe a part of Cobain's fate was caused by his disdain for God. It is written in **Matthew 12:31** that every sin can be forgiven except blasphemy. It is not my intention to demean or devalue Mr.

Cobain. I simply want to further stress the point that financial gain and success does not equate to happiness. A happy person, filled with hope and joy would not take their own life. A miserable person that cannot see through their fears, doubts, and challenges will throw away everything that has meaning to relieve themselves of pain.

I encourage you to be genuine in your desire to discover your purpose. Have a genuine faith, a genuine confidence in your gifts. I sincerely believe everyone was created with a purpose. I am bold in my proclamation that God made you for a specific reason and time. In life you are either building or destroying. You are either making things better or worse. When you figure out your place in the world, you may or may not choose to fulfill your duty. If you choose not to, be prepared for an unsatisfying life. If you choose to walk in your grace, be prepared to be great!

Any genuine philosophy leads to action and from action
back again to wonder, to the enduring fact of mystery.
-Henry Miller-

The Executioner's Execution
Play # 2 – Execute

The young man stood frozen, staring down the barrel of five rifles. The sun was scorching as the firing squad was set to execute the young thief. In this culture, stealing results in death by firing squad. As the general, responsible for giving the order to fire called out to his henchmen to fire, one did not. This soldier could not pull the trigger, sweat rolling off of his face, tears in his eyes; he knew what was to come. The next day, it was the reluctant soldier's time to die.
-The Executioner's Execution

In spring 216 B.C., Hannibal, considered one of the most exceptional strategic generals of all-time, took control of a Roman supply depot in Cannae. Hannibal had been a problem for Rome, defeating their armies in several battles. Rome decided to try a new strategy. Rome had been known for winning wars with roughly 10,000 soldiers. Legend has it that Hannibal disrupted Rome's forces to such a large extent that they sent almost 90,000 soldiers to face his army of roughly 35,000. Hannibal studied war. He was prepared for the Roman formation. When the Roman army pressed forward in battle, Hannibal used a method of retreat that deceived the Roman army into believing they were winning. However, Hannibal's army was strategically creating a circle around their enemy which led to a historic victory for the smaller army.

Achieving a desired goal begins with a vision, a purpose, and a why... but getting what you want requires a plan that is properly executed. In the Executioner's Execution, the soldier did not complete his duty. His lack of "execution" led to his death. Hannibal wanted victory and strategically played to his strengths and exposed his enemy's weaknesses. Hannibal's army attained the desired result. Your dreams, goals, or vision, will die if you fail to execute your plan.

> *"If you fail to plan properly, you will properly fail."*
> *- Ron Elliott Jr.*

MY FIRST GAME OF CHESS

I was 25 years old when I played my first game of chess. It was a rough period in my life. I'd lost everything I had and was sleeping on my childhood friend, Dub's couch. Dub's cousin, Kevin, lived in the apartment as well. Kevin was a superior chess player. I'd watch him and a few other fellas play once in a while. I'd always been intrigued by the game but never had an opponent to play. Growing up in my neighborhood, we learned to play all of the physical games— baseball, basketball, football, stickball, pick 'em up, f' em up—everything with a ball. We did not have chess boards set up at the park. Strategy for us was learning how to avoid getting jumped by the older kids.

After watching several games of chess on the smoky glass chess board, I built up the confidence to play. There was no one around to play but Kevin, so my first game was against the Jedi master of chess in the hood. I had no idea how I would defeat Kevin. Everyone that played this guy lost. I wasn't too confident in my chances but I really wanted to learn. I'd watched so many chess games take hours to play. I figured I'd at least last for 20 minutes. Kev beat me in four moves. Four freaking moves! Pawn e4, Bishop c4, Queen h5, Queen xe7, checkmate. Having a detailed plan and executing it in as few moves as possible can catapult one to success. I'd later defeated Kev once or twice, but my first game of chess taught me a lot about the necessity of a solid strategy.

The Rope-A-Dope

Recently, I'd come across an unapologetic image of Muhammad Ali towering over Floyd Mayweather. The caption read, "Who's the greatest?" The picture was created to question Floyd Mayweather's boast as the greatest fighter of all time. I'd never seen Ali fight, but I've seen clips. I've watched Floyd a few times and his defense is awesome. If you could shrink Ali, or make Floyd bigger and use a special time machine that aged each boxer in their prime, that would be a great fight!

One of the greatest stories in boxing history is Muhammad Ali's "Rope-A-Dope" strategy. It was the Rumble in the Jungle. The year was 1974 and the fight of the decade was at hand as the undefeated Heavyweight Champion of the World, George Foreman was face-to-face with the former Champion, Muhammad Ali. Some believe the Rumble in the Jungle to be the greatest sports event in history. Leading up to this monumental event, Ali had been stripped of his title and suspended from boxing for more than three years for his refusal to join the military because of his faith. Ali fought his way back into title contention but lost the "Fight of the Century" by decision to Smokin' Joe Frazier. The "Rumble in the Jungle" was Ali's chance to regain the belt.

The obvious differences between Foreman and Ali were Foreman's strength and the age difference between the two. Foreman was a fresh 25 years of age and Ali was a worn 32 years of age. Both fighters trained in Zaire (The fight was in the Congo… Africa) leading up to the fight. Foreman was the favorite. Ali had speed, the skill of a technician, and something that was overlooked that led to his victory, WISDOM. Foreman had power. Ali began the fight unusually aggressive and in close range. This was a dangerous tactic. As the fight continued, Ali unleashed his "secret plan." Ali began to lean on the ropes and let Foreman unload on him. Ali was successful at deflecting Foreman's punches and George was expending a lot of energy on the attack. Ali picked his spots. He continued to tire Foreman with his strategy.

Ali taunted Foreman… "They told me you could punch, George!" and "They told me you could punch as hard as Joe Louis." Foreman is quoted as saying, "I thought he was just one more knockout victim until, about the seventh round, I hit him hard to the jaw and he held me and whispered in my ear: 'That all you got, George?' I realized that this ain't what I thought it was."

Right hook, right hook, combo… the champ is down with nine seconds left in the round. Ali is the Heavyweight Champion of the World!

"I told you all that I was the greatest of all time… I didn't dance for a reason. I wanted him to lose all of his power, I kept telling him he had no punch. He couldn't hit, he's swinging like a sissy. He's missing, let me see you box! You can't say my legs was gone, you can't say I was tired… I stayed on the ropes. When I stayed on the ropes you thought I was doing bad but I want all boxers to put this on the page of boxing. Staying on the ropes is a beautiful thing with a heavyweight and you make him shoot his best shots and you know he's not hitting you. I would have gave George Foreman two rounds of steady punching because after that he was mine!"
– Muhammed Ali

Ali's Rope-a-Dope strategy is one for the history books. Imagine for a moment that Ali let his pride and ego come into play and he lost his cool. What if he decided that he wanted to show off his fancy footwork? What if Ali abandoned his plan? You have to learn how to strategically plan your life.

THE BIG LAUGH

Have you ever heard the saying, "If you want to make God laugh, tell Him your plans"? People often use this to shoot down your goals or dreams. But it is often misinterpreted. Sure, if you have a plan other than the path that God has chosen for you, he may laugh. But God is a proponent of FREE WILL. God is a master planner. The world has become so hardened against the truth of God that it is easy to discount the Bible as a textbook to life. I've been studying the scriptures for some time now, as well as all of the personal development experts. The same principals the "Gurus" teach you are all in the Bible.

Here is what the scripture says about planning.

Proverbs 6:6-11

[6] *Go to the ant, you sluggard;*
consider its ways and be wise!
[7] *It has no commander,*
no overseer or ruler,
[8] *yet it stores its provisions in summer*
and gathers its food at harvest.
[9] *How long will you lie there, you sluggard?*
When will you get up from your sleep?
[10] *A little sleep, a little slumber,*
a little folding of the hands to rest—
[11] *and poverty will come on you like a thief*
and scarcity like an armed man.

The ant is a simple but wise creature. The ant plans for winter in the summer. The ant diligently prepares for the time that it will be unable to provide for itself. The ant is not lazy and waiting for life to happen to it. God does not want you to be lazy.

Proverbs 21:5

[5] *The plans of the diligent lead to profit as surely haste leads to poverty.*

Pretty self-explanatory right? What about Jesus? What did Jesus have to say about planning?

Luke 14:28-30

[28] *"Suppose one of you wants to build a tower. Won't you first sit down and estimate the cost to see if you have enough money to complete it?* [29] *For if you lay the foundation and are not able to finish it, everyone who sees it will ridicule you,* [30] *saying, 'This person began to build and wasn't able to finish.'"*

Developing and executing a plan is absolutely necessary to achieving any goal. It takes time and yes it can be difficult but discovering your purpose and planning every aspect of your life according to your purpose will change your life. You will be so fulfilled when you are doing what you were created to do the right way.

ADHD

> *"The successful warrior is the average man, with laser-like focus."*
> *- Bruce Lee*

Bruce Lee was a remarkable individual. An expert martial artist and philosopher, Lee made the impossible look seamlessly possible. Known for his precision and laser like-focus, when a video of him playing ping pong with nun chucks appeared on YouTube, it was easy for people to believe that it really occurred though it was just a visual effect.

What kind of focus do you have? I am a serial entrepreneur. I always have a great idea, and I'll start a business in a heartbeat just to see how it plays out. For years I viewed this pattern as a strength. I mean, most people dream of being their own boss and I've managed to do that. Some people say, "Wow, Ron you are the ultimate hustler!" and admire the fact that I may have five things going on at the same time. Let me be clear, there is nothing wrong with having multiple streams of income, but those streams should be passive. I had a habit of actively participating in multiple businesses. "Creative ADHD," is what my condition has been referred as and it has been the demise of many great men. Over the last few years, I have been working to cure myself of this disease. There are many studies that state that multitasking is bad for the brain. You may be exceptionally gifted but until you narrow your focus, you will never achieve greatness.

A few years ago a good friend, AT, gave me a book called, *The 12 Week Year.* It is a quick read but potent. One of the lessons that stuck with me was that focusing on your plan allows you to be great at a few things rather than mediocre at many. The book challenged me to limit my goals. You do not have to conquer the world in one day. You can focus solely on improving one area of your life for a period and once you have developed the successful habits for that area, implement your plan for another area. Many of us will plan to lose 20 lbs., make a million dollars, and get a PhD in 12 weeks.

In my seminars and workshops I help participants identify, clarify, and prioritize their goals. I work with them to understand their underlying purpose and how their personality comes into play in getting what they want out of life. There are only a few areas that we must strive to master to live a happy and fulfilling life. We must plan for those areas. We need a plan for our spiritual growth. Feeding your spirit will help you endure the challenges of the world. We need a plan for our mental growth. Improving our intelligence will help us develop new ideas and add value to the marketplace. We need a plan for our money. If we do not put our dollars to work for us we squander our wealth. We need a plan for our health, personal development, professional development, and families. And executing our plans is just as important as having them.

FOCUS, FOCUS, FOCUS!

Consequence

There is a story of a prophet in the Bible. This prophet was told by God to go see the king of Israel and inform him that he would die. God told the prophet to speak his peace and keep moving. The prophet was not to stay, eat, or drink. The king obviously did not like being told that his reign was going to end unfavorably. First he threatened the prophet, but that did not work out too well. His hand became frozen. The prophet prayed for his release and the king begged the prophet to stay and offered him gifts. The prophet rightfully declined and left the city. An older prophet in the city found out about the young prophet and invited him to stay and eat with him.

The younger man of God declined but his elder said, "God came to me and told me that you were to come to my home and eat and drink with me." The young man complied and went to the older prophet's home. God then came to the elder and gave him this message: "Tell the young prophet that he will not be buried with his people because he disobeyed me." The prophet left to go home and on the road was killed by a lion.

Reward

Yeshua (Jesus) fasted for 40 days and 40 nights. After his time in the wilderness, Satan came to him and tempted him. Satan tempted Yeshua to prove that he was the Son of God. He offered him the kingdoms of the earth and all of the riches of the world. Yeshua declined. And according to the scriptures sits at the right hand of the Father.

The prophet was killed by the lion and Jesus became the lion. When you focus you will be rewarded. When you do not focus on your plan it will die. You do not want your dream to die but it will if you fail to execute. Execution is the "Action" part of your strategy. You've created the plan and now it is time to implement the tactics that will help you reach your end game. You have identified your purpose and it is time to DO SOMETHING to GET IT. Champions are made by executing.

A contemporary of mine that works with youth uses a great acronym to encourage young people. To achieve your "dreams" you must D.R.E.A.M. You have to be Dedicated and Responsible. Educate yourself and have the right Attitude. Finally, you have to Motivate yourself. Why? It's your dream. What you want to "GET" is not limited by your age, race, circumstance, or environment. Success does not happen by accident. I love SMART goals. There are many goal setting frameworks that help you stay on task. SMART goals are one of my go to strategies when helping a client create a clear picture of what they want to do. When your goals are Specific, Measurable, Attainable, Relevant, and Time-Bound... they are more likely to happen. Sticking with your goals, focusing on your DREAM and being SMART will prevent your dreams from meeting the fate of the Executioner.

JUST DO IT!

Nike is easily the most recognized sports brand in the world. The Swoosh is a universal symbol and "Just Do It" is a cultural statement that will live forever. Think about it; I bet you a pair of imitation Jordan's (just in case I'm wrong... lol) that you cannot instantly think of the slogan of any other athletic wear brand. What is Adidas' slogan? Reebok? What about Under Armor? Nike has become an expert of execution. Nike has a cultural brand. The most effective strategy Nike has used is aligning its brand with the best, with champions. Champions do what is needed to win. Here is a short list of champions affiliated with Nike:

1. Michael Jordan
2. Kobe Bryant
3. LeBron James
4. Serena Williams
5. Tiger Woods
6. Drew Brees
7. Alex Rodriguez

All of the above are championship athletes. All have a reputation for doing what it takes to win. Nike has created a culture that is supported by aligning its brand with individuals that embody their slogan, "Just Do It!" I want you to develop the heart of a champion. Ali said he was the greatest. I want you to be the greatest you. See it in your mind. See yourself healthy. See yourself wealthy. See yourself making a difference. See yourself enjoying your family. See yourself living your dream. You have to see it in your mind before you can do it.

A Champion's Heart

I won't rest until I claim the prize
I dream about the trophy ever night
I will play through the pain
I'm on when I am off

in the off-season I train

When there is no one to cheer me on

I will motivate myself

I will not run from the challenge

I overcome adversity, I crush doubt

It is bigger than me

It is more than a game

My heart does not pump fear

My mind stays on the game

I am always thinking about the win

I respect my opponents, they are worthy

but I want it more…

I enjoy the moment

I desire success

I desire to leave a legacy

The heart of a champion

STOP READING RIGHT NOW...

Find a mirror right now and tell yourself, "I have the victory!!! I am a champion!!!!" Doesn't that feel great? You may not believe it but you are a champion. Yes, you are a champion! You are a champion because you are taking the time right now to read this book. Reading is the Education part of your DREAM. Most accomplished people attribute their success to their personal library. The GET IT framework is based on the habits of winners. Applying the knowledge from this book will help you get everything you want. Believe in yourself! Be genuine and create the life you want. The greats expect to perform well because of the blood, sweat, and tears they have invested in preparation. The mental work of motivating yourself is a huge part of executing. Do the work. Go for the win. EXECUTE.

Victory

Do you know what Nike means? Nike is a Greek word for "Victory." Nike's math is simple: Just Do It. Get the Victory. I believe your victory is waiting for you. It does not matter if it is an academic victory, an emotional victory, a sports victory, a financial victory, or victory in any other area of life. Your victory is waiting for you to take it. When I was younger, I used to watch a show called, "In Living Color." In Living Color was a sketch comedy show created by the extremely talented and funny family, the Wayans. There was a character played by David Allen Grier by the name of Calhoun Tubbs. Calhoun Tubbs was a musician that had a song for every situation. Before he would share his songs, he would tell a story and then say, "Wrote a song about it; want to hear it? Here it go!" I encourage you to visit YouTube to get the full experience. Here is my Calhoun Tubbs moment.

I have been fortunate in life to be blessed with many gifts. One of those gifts is music. I am a professional hobbyist. There is no doubt in my mind that if I wanted to be a professional recording artist, I could. However, I believe I can be much more effective in the capacity as an author, speaker, and trainer. "Industry rule number 4080: record company people are shady!!!" A famous quote from Q-Tip of A Tribe Called Quest has held true during my tenure as a recording artist.

I just was not a fan of the music business. I enjoy my new life as a hobbyist. My daughter has now picked up the torch in the pursuit of happiness. She's writing songs, singing, and performing. As for me, I write a song every now and again just for fun. I wrote a song about victory, titled, "NYKE." NYKE means Nearing Your Kingdom of Excellence. Music is a great tool for confession and affirmation. NYKE is featured on the GET IT soundtrack. The soundtrack is a supplemental component to help you stay motivated in times when you may not be able to pick up this book. The lyrics are life changing and you should adopt them as a part of your everyday life. "Wrote a song about it; want to hear it??? Here it go!"

NYKE (Chorus)

I got the victory
I can't accept defeat
I see the finish line
Gotta stay on my grind
Gotta stay on my toes
I am my only foe
Their ain't no competition
No one can stop me, NO!
I'm on my NYKE, Heir

An "Heir" is the person next up to rule the throne. You are Nearing Your Kingdom of Excellence with every successful tactic that you implement. Even your failures are building blocks for your kingdom because they are lessons that allow you to grow. You are next up to rule. You are the heir to the throne. When "Victory" is on your lips, the only thing that can prevent you from winning is you. You are your only competition. When you do not position yourself to win, you allow yourself to lose. Overcome yourself. Eradicate the doubt and fear. Focus on your strengths. Use what you have to cross the finish line. Start with the end in mind. Remember, See It, Believe It, Achieve It. Envision yourself with the prize, the trophy, the ring. Tell yourself right now, "I have the heart of a champion. I have the victory. I execute the master plan and will win."

Execution happens first in the mind. I want you to take a minute and imagine a stadium filled with cheering fans chanting your name. See yourself making your victory lap waving to your adoring fans. Visualization is a powerful tool. Doing something in your mind before it manifests in the body is a common thread in the lives of successful people. Do what the winners do. It is OK if you feel uncomfortable. Comfortable people do not grow, they stay the same.

A Fair Warning

Doing what it takes is a matter of doing a series of little things. Develop the little habits that provide great results. From time to time I get a client that is not getting the results they want quickly enough. When this occurs, I teach them about Process Goals. Often we get so stuck on your Product Goal or end goal that we do not celebrate the little victories that get us there. Process goals are the little goals that add up to the Product Goal. Master the process. If you want to lose 20 pounds, understand the science behind it and set little goals that add up to the BIG ONE. What does losing 20 pounds look like? First, being specific, I want to lose 20 pounds in ten weeks. I will exercise for 30 minutes, 7 days per week. I will eliminate bread, processed foods, and sugar from my meal plan. I will sleep eight hours every night. And I will document what I eat every day to hold myself accountable. Accomplishing these small goals will end in losing 20 pounds.

Being a Go Getter means you will get the job done. If you have to wake up early, wake up. If you have to go to bed late, stay awake. If you want to be the best shooter on your team, shoot more shots. If you want to be a better wife, spend more time catering to your husband's needs. You may have to do activities you hate. You might have to work with people you do not like. You must do what is necessary to get what you want. Everything you want in life comes at some expense. Be prepared to pay the price. Do not complain about the costs. Make sure you can afford it before you break the bank, figuratively and literally. Learn to be ok with failure. When things do not go as planned, adjust the plan! Do things the right way, focus on the win, stay dedicated, and realize your dreams. Just Do It! The only true failure is the failure to act.

Execution is Key

So how do we ensure that we execute? First we must develop a plan. We must create a vision, create a mission, and set a goal. There are a lot of ways to create attainable goals. At the heart of them all is stating clearly what you want. Let's take a look at a few goal setting frameworks and see how they can be integrated in your plan for achieving a life of balance and success.

Product/Process Goals

Product and Process Goals are likely one of the simplest goal setting frameworks one can apply. I was first introduced to this framework when I became a fitness professional. I have found it to be very effective with short term goals.

Product Goals are end goals. For example, if you say I want to lose twenty pounds, you have just set a Product Goal. This is only the first step in attaining this goal. A Product Goal without a Process Goal is like the sky without the sun.

Process Goals are the actual execution parts of the end goal. The process is the who, what, when, where and how. The process for losing twenty pounds could include a change in how one eats, more exercise, or even getting more sleep. The process is the little steps you take daily to reach your end goal.

If you are not a detailed person and need a quick way to set a goal, the Product/Process Goal setting protocol is a great way to start. There is one thing this framework ignores; your "Why." And remember, "Why" is super important because it will be what helps you to stay on task. If you know your why and it is strong enough, the Product/Process model may be perfect for you.

SMART GOALS

Common knowledge to some, new to others, SMART GOALS, are a highly effective way of putting plans in action. What I like about SMART GOALS is that they have the why built into the framework. How do we set a SMART goal?

First we must understand what being **SMART** means…

S-Specific
M-Measurable
A-Attainable

R-Relevant
T-Time Bound

When you set a goal, be clear about what it is you want to attain. To say, "I just want to make more money" is not specific. A specific goal would be:

I want to make $100,000 in six months.

The above goal is very specific as well as measurable. The only way to know if we are being effective in life is if we keep track of our results. When we keep track of our results we are more equipped to make the necessary adjustments when we fall short as well as track what is really working. Is the goal of making $100,000 in six months measurable? Yes! Why? It is measurable because it is a figure. We know that we achieved success if we reach that number in six months. Now I do not know about you, but if one set this goal and it took nine months I highly doubt they would complain.

Is making a $100,000 in six months attainable? Well, this is subjective. If you have the type of capital (idea or capital) that allows you to do big business, yes. However, if you are an hourly worker at Wendy's, no.

Relevancy is our "Why." Why I want or need to make $100,000 in six months will determine my effort. If my "why" is weak, my effort will surely follow the same path. We live in a world of vanity. Our society is like James Bond movie titles. Because of the Skyfall, we wish we had a Goldfinger. We have no idea how to come up on that Goldfinger so we hit the Casino Royale. If we are embracing our "English" heritage and strike out at the Casino we play the Thunderball hoping to win a boatload of cash, affording us diamonds. Diamonds are Forever, and YOLO isn't true because You Only Live Twice. However, you may not believe that Dr. No, but you know nothing at all except the World Isn't Enough. All that is a fancy way of saying we want a lot of things in life that are really of little significance. What good is a hundred-thousand-dollar car, if you have a terminal illness? What is success without someone to share it with? Make sure your goal passes the "Why" test.

It does not take a rocket scientist to recognize that our goal is time bound. I will discuss "Time" in great detail in Chapter 5. As it applies to our goal, we've set an end date. This date will allow us another metric to measure our success. Placing a time on a goal also increases the urgency as we realize what must be done to accomplish the goal within that designated time.

In review of our goal of making $100,000 in six months, the way to improve this goal and ensure that it is truly smart is to add the "why" to the statement.

I want to make $100,000 in six months so I can fund my children's college fund. This becomes a SMART goal because now it is Relevant. SMART goals are an excellent place to start when taking the journey to success. This framework provides a simple blueprint to design the life you want.

GET IT GOALS

The GET IT goal framework was created out of a desire to achieve my personal goals. I took notice that successful people all followed a uniformed code of sorts. Despite their different walks of life, the principles they apply to life are virtually the same. GET IT goals take in account the macros of success. This framework is about a bigger picture, bigger than just achieving a goal, but more about creating a life, a movie worth millions seeing, or even better, a masterpiece for an audience of one. So how do we GET IT?

We've covered the G, being Genuine about your faith, your desires, and purpose is essential to attain and maintain any level of success.

The fact that you are reading this book and studying the principles is a part of your Execution. You have to become informed before you can develop a strategy. Knowledge properly applied is Power. When you know what your purpose is, and you create a strategy to fulfill it, your chances of DOING IT have increased greatly. I have had so many ideas that I did not capitalize on. Some of which others ran with and were very successful. Execution is all about commitment. Commit to your success and you will achieve it.

Tact is a strategic tool. You will learn about the importance of the approach in the next chapter. If being Genuine embodies our "why" and Execution our "what," then Tact is a huge part of our "How." Tact is a skill that can be developed by anyone over time. Most successful people use it and employ strategic tactics to achieve what they want out of life.

Another tool, and a really huge part of our how is Intelligence. Intelligence plays a gigantic part in achieving success. Intelligence has multiple dimensions such as acquired knowledge, natural gifts, research, and developed talents. Learning to use what you have to get what you want is the idea and winners are great at employing what they do best to get results.

Lastly in this framework is the concept of time. Time must be valued. It is about priorities. In the chapter about Time you will learn how precious it is and why you should take advantage of every moment. Successful people do not waste time, they value it and you should too!

As you can see, where **PRODUCT/PROCESS** goals and **SMART** goals deal with microcosms of success, **GET IT** goals focus on the big picture. It is important to utilize all forms because they work together to create a beautiful image called, Your Life. You can create the life you want. You can be happy. You can enjoy your family and provide for them. You can do the things you love and help the people you love. You can GET IT! Get it?

VISUALIZATION

The last thing I want to cover in this chapter is the power and importance of visualization and confession. I believe seeing what you want is important in achieving it. I do not mean pretend that you already have it, that will do a disservice to you. However, closing your eyes and seeing yourself doing what it is you intended to do will help you to achieve it. In basketball, a great shooter shoots the shot before the ball ever leaves her hands. She sees the ball going just over the rim. Champions see the crowd going crazy after a big goal before the goal is even scored. Visualizing your success is necessary to build your belief. Some will argue that it will make you lazier and more comfortable. I can agree with that sentiment if all you do is fantasize, but if you focus your visualization routine on building the faith you need to achieve I am certain the results will follow.

Similar to Visualization, Confession is an important tool to help you execute your goals as well. Confession, slightly different than affirmation, is more spiritually based rather than psychology based. Confession is the matter of speaking what God spoke. God called those that believe to be blessed, so if you believe, you should only say that you are blessed. God said He created you for a purpose, your mouth should embrace that as well. At the center of everything I've been sharing is the fact that God created us for a purpose. I do not believe true success can be attained apart from that purpose. If you want to really execute the goals and dreams that you desire, make the vision plain and do not let corrupt communication come out of your mouth. Think about a boat, a very small thing called a rudder steers and turns the boat. Your tongue steers the rudder of your life. If you want to turn things in your favor, see them the way you want them to be, speak them, plan them, and execute them.

Tee It Up
Play # 3 – Tact

All men can see these tactics whereby I conquer, but what none
can see is the strategy out of which victory is evolved.
–Sun Tzu

Tact is the ability to describe others as they see themselves.
–Abraham Lincoln

The Approach

In golf, the approach is the shot that a player plays to get the ball from
the fairway onto the greens. It is usually a long shot and requires a full
swing. In life our approach also helps us close the gap between where
we currently stand and our goals. It is rare in golf for anyone to hit
a hole in one from the fairway. It is also rare in life that we achieve
everything we want without building great relationships. The irony
of this analogy is that many deals are closed on the golf course.

I cannot say that I was a fan of golf. I did watch it from time to time, but it's like baseball to me, boring unless you are there. I never had much interest in the game, but one day an organization that I was a member of decided to arrange lessons for us and I wanted to try something new. The first thing I learned was that it is much more difficult than it looks. Second, I learned how relaxing it was. I immediately fell in love with the sport on a personal level. I'm still not very good, but I enjoy the game. The course is also a great place to network and get deals done.

"The Donald," the billionaire real estate mogul, told Golf.com that the golf course was a place that helped him close many deals and gain access to people that he would not normally have accessed. Granted, Trump is wealthy and likely is invited to join private clubs with other wealthy individuals, still his line of thinking is easily adopted. His approach is simple: Find people that can further the cause and go where they are.

Life is not a solo sport. Life is nothing without relationships. Having awesome, mutually beneficial relationships requires tact. Tact, the root word of tactics which I discussed in the previous chapter, is critical in getting the things you want out of life. Though cliché, the statement, "It's not what you know but who you know" is eerily true. More importantly, it is not about who you know, but who knows you and how they feel about you. If you want to live life at a higher level, a higher vibration, then help others feel great about themselves. You'd be amazed at what a smile can do, or the impact a kind word to a stranger can have. You can know what you are supposed to do, have a well thought out plan, and be passionate about making it happen, but without people to share in the experience, those things become obsolete.

It is important that you develop an approach. Not just an approach with people, but an approach with life. Govern yourself with a code, a mission statement. Approach life with a winning attitude. Life will throw curveball after curveball and might even hit you upside the head from time to time, but if you learn to manage yourself and be level headed, it will never strike you out.

I remember reading about the famed world champion chess player, Bobby Fischer. On the account of anyone that witnessed him play, he was considered a genius. In 1972, Fischer defeated another champion, Boris Spassky, by changing his approach. Chess is a game steeped in strategy and tactics. Spassky was a real champion and known for his levelheaded play. In fact, Spassky had defeated Fischer every time they played until this championship series. Spassky won because he played on his opponent's predictability and defeated them at their own game. Bobby Fischer learned the key to defeating his nemesis had more to do with his ways off of the board rather than on it. Fischer created a "rope-a-dope" strategy similar to that of Ali's versus George Foreman. Fischer refused to play, showed up late, and lost a game on purpose to position himself for the ultimate victory. During the series, Spassky knew Fischer had a trick up his sleeve but could not figure it out. Fischer throwing a game was to feed Spassky's ego, to make him feel unbeatable and to prove that he was unpredictable. Fischer's use of tact, or lack of it, disrupted his opponent's strategy and led to Fischer's victory.

I am not a proponent of deceit and trickery. I believe you can do things straight up and honest to receive your rewards. But it is important that you understand the various ways this play works. In a game of chess, being deceptive is permissible and doesn't lead to any consequences away from the game. In real life, I recommend against using deceitful tactics.

Get Rich or Die Trying

"Understand: people judge you by appearances, the image you project through your actions, words, and style. If you do not take control of this process, then people will see and define you the way they want to, often to your detriment. You might think that being consistent with this image will make others respect and trust you, but in fact it is the opposite— over time you seem predictable and weak. Consistency is an illusion anyway—each passing day brings changes within you. You must not be afraid to express these evolutions. The powerful learn early in life that they have the freedom to mold their image, fitting the needs and moods of the moment. In this way, they keep others off balance and maintain an air of mystery. You must follow this path and find great pleasure in reinventing yourself, as if you were the author writing your own drama."
– 50 Cent, The 50th Law

50 Cent (Curtis Jackson) has always intrigued me. His path to success is an unlikely one. 50's mom was a young coke dealer that was murdered when he was only eight years old. By the age of twelve he was following in his mother's footsteps. 50 was arrested in 10th grade for bringing a gun and drugs to school. In 1994, Curtis was sentenced to 3-9 years after being arrested again for narcotics and weapons. Fast forward to modern times and Mr. Jackson is said to have a net worth north of $150 M.

How does a young Black male, from Southside Queens overcome the loss of his mother, the ills of the dope game, being shot 9 times, and blackballed in the music industry to become a respected business mogul? Tact. 50 Cent's philosophy, strategy, tactical implementation, and relationships helped 50 amass his fortune. In he and Robert Greene's book "The 50th Law," 50 attributes a portion of his ability to navigate through the world to "intense realism." Intense realism means accepting things for what they are and living in the moment. Instead of wishing things were different or working in your favor, become better and adapt to the reality at hand. This approach is powered by focus. Living in the moment is a difficult task when life is giving you lemons. It is much easier to imagine sitting on a beach in Puerto Rico with a tall glass of ice cold lemonade than to take the lemons and make lemonade without sugar.

Another thing 50 did, that all extremely successful people do is to disassociate with people that are not moving in the same upward direction. It has been said that you are the sum total of the five people you spend the most time with. Separating yourself from your friends and family can be difficult. Finding new friends and relationships with individuals sharing the same goals and mind state will propel and motivate you to achieve your objectives. Spending more time with your contemporaries does not mean unfriending or loving your friends or family less, it just means you have to challenge yourself by creating strategic relationships and partnerships that force you to grow.

My basketball journey began on the hard concrete pavements of Detroit. O'Hare Park had a crack filled, uneven playing surface with a steel, bullet hole filled, backboard. There was only one rim, no nets and a lot of forty ounce beers. Getting a game on this court was difficult because all of the drug dealers and gangsters from the surrounding neighborhoods had a monopoly on the court. I had an ace in hole, my older brother was the neighborhood basketball and baseball star and just so happened to be a street guy. My brother's rep got me a spot on the court. I was pushed around, taunted, and knocked down. I had my shots blocked and ball stolen. Faced with adversity, I learned to adjust. I became stronger. I became quicker. I practiced dribbling more, shooting more... I became better because I played with people better than me. When I played with people my age, I dominated them. Some had equal skill and talent, but the mental edge was always mine. You must adopt the winner's mentality if you are to get everything you want out of life. Everything has a price. Sometimes that price is letting go of things or people that will keep you from your purpose.

Strategic Alliances

50 Cent was blackballed by the recording industry. He'd made fun of popular artists, been shot, and lost a deal. His rise to the top was a result of several effective tactics. First, he had a team. They worked hard creating a lot of mixtape material. Secondly, he gave his music to the bootleggers to make him hot in the street. In the early 2000s, the mixtape game was where it was at and 50 Cent was at the forefront of it. 50's mixtape landed in the hands of Eminem, who brought 50 to Dr. Dre, and BOOM... "You can find me in the club..." was being played in every club and radio station in the world. Relationships are everything. There is no product without a customer. There is no mentor with a mentee. No teacher without a student. No moon without the sun. 50 Cent's fearless approach to life, tenacity, and street smarts put him in the room with rap royalty. *Get Rich or Die Tryin'* sold millions of copies, making 50 the international star and businessman he is today.

When the Music Stops

When the records stopped playing, Curtis did not. 50 used his celebrity to build brands. His most lucrative deal came with Vitamin Water. Because 50 was such a high risk artist, he had to give up a higher percentage of his music profits to obtain his record deal. To make up for the lost revenues, 50 Cent's management team worked diligently to align him with popular brands through endorsement deals. One of those deals was with Reebok.

Chris Lighty, 50 Cent's manager, suggested that 50 Cent take a swig of Vitamin Water at the end of a Reebok commercial. 50 had been introduced to the beverage by a personal trainer. At this point in time, he had not been paid a dime to endorse the sports drink. Chris Lighty was thinking ahead. An old business associate, Rohan Oza, worked with Lighty and Sprite on the "Obey Your Thirst" campaign with A Tribe Called Quest. Lighty was hoping to catch Oza's attention with the Reebok spot and did. Oza happened to be the brand manager for Glaceau, the company that created Vitamin Water. After seeing the commercial, Rohan set up a meeting with the company and 50 Cent. The irony of the relationship is that the company's headquarters was in Queens where 50 grew up. Allegedly, that meeting resulted in a deal giving 50 a $5M fee and 5% equity in the company.

The "Formula 50" campaign made Vitamin Water a top contender in the sports drink industry worldwide with approximately 30 percent of the United States' market share. Vitamin Water's success was mainly attributed to 50's worldwide brand as an entertainer. Coca Cola took notice of Glaceau and purchased the company for 4.1 billion dollars, cash. This purchase made 50 Cent approximately $200M before taxes of course. No need to die trying, 50 was really rich.

You may not be as business savvy as a 50 Cent, but you can develop a strategy for every area of your life to help you achieve your goals. It is written in Proverbs 4:7, "Wisdom is the principal thing; therefore get wisdom: and with all thy getting get understanding." Operating with tact is a matter of acquiring wisdom and applying it to your life. In every situation, good, bad, or indifferent is a lesson. It is our job to learn from those lessons and to use what we learn to get what we desire.

ROC-A-FELLA YALL!

One of, if not the richest man of his time, John Davison Rockefeller Sr. was a wise businessman. Mr. Rockefeller began his journey into industry at the age of 16. At the age of 20, the young man had built a merchant business that had grossed almost ½ million dollars. Rockefeller's intuition led him into the oil business in the early 1860s. His intuition proved to be on the money. John's oil company, Standard Oil became the largest, most successful oil company in the United States. The company was so prosperous that the Congress of the United States brought an antitrust lawsuit against the oil monopoly. Rockefeller had built a company that owned almost every aspect of the oil business. Standard owned refineries, pipelines, and land to prevent competition. Rockefeller was a tactical genius. After the suit was brought upon Standard Oil, he dissolved the corporation and allowed each property to operate under the name, while still in his control. After amassing an unimaginable amount of wealth,

Rockefeller retired at 56 and lived the rest of his life as a philanthropist giving away over $530 million to various causes.

Over a century later, a new Roc-A-Fella emerged amassing a net worth almost equal to the philanthropic efforts of the original Rockefeller. Shawn Corey Carter, known to the world as Jay Z is one of the best-selling artists of all-time. Growing up in Brooklyn, New York and raised in Marcy Houses projects, Jay Z has risen like the Phoenix to be an American icon. According to the Jigga man, he came into the rap game wealthy from selling a new form of oil, "crack cocaine."

"I came into this game a 100 grand strong/Nine to be exact from grindin' G packs/put this thing in motion ain't no rewindin' back/can make 40 off a brick but one rhyme can beat that..."
- Jay Z

In the 80s, the drug trade made a lot young black men wealthy. It was not sustainable wealth and Jay Z recognizing this decided to use another skill he developed to "rape Def Jam" till he was the $100 million man. Roc-A-Fella Records was founded by Jay Z, Dame Dash, and Kareem "Biggs" Burke. The company was created because no label would sign the talented Mr. Carter. The three young CEOs put up their own money to create one of Hip Hop's most respected dynasties.

"I got my swagger back..."
- Jay Z

Jay Z learned early in his career that he had the ear of young people. If he said, "I eat dog food." a million kids would start eating dog food. He and his partners capitalized on the power of their brand by entering into the clothing business and exploiting endorsement deals from some of the biggest brands in the world from Budweiser to Reebok.

A Kingdom Divided

Dame Dash was from Harlem and Jay from Brooklyn. Dame was the deal maker and Jay the deal keeper. They were the perfect blend of fire and ice. Dame's passion however was a gift and a curse for the young businessman. Dame was known for being loud and difficult. Other men with Dame's characteristics would be heralded, but a young man that built his company from the ground up without support is threatening to an established organization. Over the course of Roc-A-Fella's tenure with Def Jam, Dame managed to step on too many toes and the powers that be were ready for a change. The change came when Dame, Biggs, and Jay decided to sell the remaining equity of Roc-A-Fella Records to Def Jam for $10M. Dame previously mentioned the possibility of a sale under the assumption that he'd still run the company. When the guns blazed and the smoke cleared, Jay Z was the President of Def Jam, Dame was out and the end of an era was cemented. Friends became foes beyond a Reasonable Doubt... all pun intended.

Excuse Me Mr. President

President Carter's run at Def Jam was short lived but it increased his stronghold in the music industry. During his presidency, the god MC helped artists such as Rihanna, Rick Ross, Young Jeezy, and Kanye West explode into superstardom and establish their own music empires. Jay Z was determined to introduce the world to Mr. Carter, the businessman.

"I'm not a businessman. I'm a business, man!"
-Jay Z

Imagine growing up poor in the projects during the Crack Era, selling drugs, escaping, becoming a music superstar, and the CEO of the most notable Hip Hop label in history. Additionally, your influence and fame rises to the extent that you have the President of the United States' ear. Mr. Carter learned the art of politicking at a young age and used this crucial skill to propel him to a net worth of more than a half of billion dollars. While his former partner, Dame Dash was fire, Jay remained cool as ice. The person that is cold and calculated operates with a level of tact that far exceeds those that are led solely by passion. It is imperative for you to use your passion to drive your vision and maintain a cool and collected posture to achieve your goals. Shawn Carter never graduated from high school, overcame immeasurable odds, and has dinner at the White House occasionally with his beautiful superstar wife, Beyoncé. If this kid from Brooklyn can hurdle the piles of excuses, setbacks, environmental conditions, and lack of formal education to become a top influencer in popular culture in every arena from media to politics... YOU CAN TOO!

"Boy from the hood but got White House Clearance."
- Jay Z

Tactician

A tactician is someone that is good at making plans in order to achieve a goal. From a military standpoint, a tactician is skilled at organizing his military forces, strategizing, and implementing the right use of weapons to achieve victory. You are the tactician for your life. The resources to succeed are in your hands. Your forces are your relationships. Your weapons are your gifts. Similar to 50 Cent or Jay Z, you can create your approach for a hole in one victory. Live a limitless life. Spend as much time as necessary studying the success of others in your field, or people succeeding in what you'd like to succeed in. If you want to be a great wife, study and learn from other great wives. If you want to be a great chef, study and learn from great chefs. Study greatness, create your own secret sauce, and become great.

Setting goals and planning are skills needed for success in every area of life. Developing a solid strategy is imperative to attain your goal. If you have a vision in your mind, a purpose in your heart, and you have tried to bring it into fruition but have failed to do so, it is likely because you did not first create a written plan of action. If you have not identified your target, recruited your troops and organized them, it will not be possible to win the war of life. You must have also mastered your weapons. Extensive weapons and combat training will keep you alive in the heat of the battle. Whether you believe it or not, you have a strategy. Your strategy is either effective or ineffective. Becoming a great strategist comes with practice and patience. And most importantly, knowing the rules of engagement for the game you play. Every game has different rules. In mastering one game you will have developed the ability to apply the process to any game but you will still have to learn the new angles of each area of life. Often we fail because we attempt to use a "blanket philosophy" or apply a "one size fits all" type of strategy to everything we do.

The Wrong Race

A young and talented runner trained harder, studied champions, woke up early, went to bed late dreaming about his chance to win a big race. He was faster and stronger than the competition. The day was soon approaching that he would compete with the best. He had to apply to participate in the race but was not too interested in filling out the application himself so he asked his mother to do it for him. His mother was a very busy lady, had other kids, worked, but she'd do anything for her favorite child. There were two types of athletes competing in the race. One type was the typical able bodied participants and the other type were athletes with disabilities. The application for the athletes with disabilities stated in the title, "Future Special Olympian." The mother, believing that her child was so special, completed the application and sent it in proud that her son would possibly become a future Olympic star.

The day of the event, the young man went to his designated registration table, signed in and prepared for competition. When it was time for his race, the athletes were summoned to the track. At the starting line, he noticed that some of the kids had prosthetic legs and some others had conditions that he was not sure about. But in his mind he was excited for them because he saw the confidence in their eyes. He was happy they were overcoming their disabilities and competing with "normal" kids like him. The race began, our "Future Special Olympian" sprinted out the gate and ran to victory ousting the competition. After the race the announcer said into the loudspeaker, "Congrats to the winner of our **Future Special Olympian** 100M Race, now get ready for our **Future Olympian** 100M Race." The young man won, but he ran the wrong race. His celebration ended in disappointment.

Often we do not narrow our focus enough to develop the skill of goal setting. We find ourselves working jobs that we hate. We find ourselves unfulfilled. It is not that we cannot win, but we are running the wrong race. We are playing the wrong game. We are not walking the path that was intended for us to walk. The first play of this playbook was to be Genuine. To be genuine you must know "who" you are and "why" you are. Once you know "who" you are and "why" you are then you can develop your strategy and execute with tactical precision. All of the gentlemen that I have mentioned thus far have mastered these steps. Another common denominator in the lives of winners is that they build strong teams.

Mastermind

Draft day is a major day in the National Basketball Association. The team with the number one pick is looking for the best player to improve their team. The ownership and coaches are looking to add value to their organization. They scout and recruit throughout the entire world to find a player with the right skill set to assist them in their ultimate goal of winning a championship. In life, you are the player, as well as the owner of your organization. You are the CEO of your brand. From a player's perspective, you must develop your skills to increase your value before you can build a team around you. When a team wins a game in the NBA, there are fans, cheerleaders, coaches and trainers doing everything they can to help their team win. If the team is not good, or not putting forth an effort, their support diminishes drastically. Therefore, before developing your mastermind, you must be a master of self and be attractive to the marketplace.

Now that you know your purpose, now that you know your strong "why," it is possible to build your brand in a manner that entices others to join your cause. Here are five tips to help ensure your brand is maximizing its marketability for the development of a mastermind.

1. Your Passion must be evident.
2. You must Genuinely care about people.
3. You must Know who you are and what you want.
4. You must be Friendly.
5. You must make yourself Unforgettable.

Once you have proven to be attractive, you are ready to create your mastermind group. The purpose of the mastermind is to help you stay sharp, to help you build a network, and to position you to benefit from the relationships of those in your group. We have always been taught, "Birds of a feather flock together." Maybe you have heard, "you are the sum total of the five people with whom you spend the most time." If you spend time with people that think small, you will tend to think small. It is of the utmost importance that you find a way to add value to people that are smarter than you and more connected than you.

Think of your mastermind group as an All-Star lineup. Imagine that you are the Avengers. Everyone on your team has something to bring to the table and is there to push each other to be the best they can be. Select people that motivate and inspire you to be great. Provide reciprocity and strive to do the same.

There are four types of groups you can create.

1. Accountability Group
2. Like Interest Group
3. Cause Based Group
4. Investment Group

Let's take a look at these four groups.

Accountability

In 2010, I decided to make a push to get back into shape. Marriage and fatherhood can change a man's habits for better or worse. In my case, it was for worse. I wanted to achieve the highest fitness level possible, so I ordered P90X. My sudden motivation was really inspired by an upcoming trip to Disney World. I was looking at a picture of my daughter and I in the pool and my belly was like that of a pregnant woman. I did not want to take another picture with a big fat belly. It was time to get to work.

P90X was hard, to say the least. I struggled through the first month but made sure I pressed play every single day. I completed the program and had tremendous results. I enjoyed it so much that I ordered the next program, Insanity. When Insanity came I felt like I could do anything because P90X was so difficult. To my surprise Insanity was a new level of difficulty. I started, but did not finish. Every few months over the course of two and a half years that would be my relationship with the program.

In the fall of 2012, my wife ordered a program and seemed to be sticking with it. She was dedicated to getting in shape. I watched and quickly became motivated to attempt Insanity one more time. My wife's friends had an online group to help inspire and motivate each other. We joined the group and with the help of the members of the group, we both completed our programs because we had the social support that I learned later as a fitness professional was of the utmost importance. Accountability groups are intended to help you reach a goal. In our group, we posted our meals, recorded our workouts, and checked in with each other to make sure we were staying on track. This type of mastermind group is essential if you find yourself struggling to remain focused on completing a task.

Like Interest

My wife and I are blessed to be a part of the 2% club. What's the 2% club? We are parents of twins. Twins make up approximately 2% of the United States population. As a result of having twins, my wife has been proactive in joining online communities for parents with multiples. This type of mastermind is based on the topic. In these groups, women share their experiences with each other in hopes to learn from each other and to find comfort.

Caused Based

Caused based or Mission based groups are often formed by a group of people desiring to achieve a single goal. This type of group is popular amongst those with political aims.

Investment Based

Investment based groups are designed with the premise of helping the individuals in the group grow their businesses.

Mastermind Success

Your goal is to create a group that embodies all four types of groups. You may even have three or four different groups. The idea is to develop mutually beneficial relationships. La Costra Nostra was a great example of what a mastermind group should be. Charles "Lucky" Luciano was brilliant (though criminal) in his idea to bring order and corporate structure to the Mob. Lucky gave every leader a seat at the table eliminating the need for competition. When bringing people together, it is important to establish the purpose for the union and to make sure everyone has bought into the purpose. In the case of the Mob, the commission was put into place to help everyone make more money and have less headaches. What is your purpose for organizing your group? You must define this purpose in the form of a mission statement.

My personal mission statement is:

To build a home, teach a class, and start a revolution. To edify and encourage millions to discover their purpose and live it with passion and let their lives speak volumes.

For me to be build a successful team, I must make sure that they agree and are committed to my purpose. If a member of your group or team is not fully committed to the mission, failure will be the result.

If commitment to the purpose is the first step to achieving mastermind success, the second step would be establishing clear expectations. When my wife and I were first married we experienced a lot of interpersonal problems. We argued often and most times it was over trivial things. Our first three years were burdensome, full of stress, and we both had doubts about the union we formed. As I grew spiritually, I worked hard to find a resolve. I attended counselling, spent a lot of time in prayer, and gave my best effort to remain at peace with my wife. In my time of enlightenment, I discovered that most of our marital problems were a result of our expectations of each other. Prior to marriage, we never discussed what we expected from each other. In turn, we clashed like the Titans.

Setting expectations of team members is a critical element of success. When you dissect championship basketball teams you will notice that each player has a role, knows his/her role, and fulfills that role. As the coach for your life, you must put people in the positions of your life that will allow them to best use their gifts and talents to help you achieve your goals. When 50 Cent inked the Vitamin Water deal, it was not just his celebrity that made it happen, it was his team.

Picking your team is just like the NBA draft. You want to know the strengths and weaknesses of those you surround yourself with. You want to know their character flaws, vices, their passions, ambitions, fears, and anything you can utilize to help them reach their maximum potential. You want to protect them from destructive behavior and push them to greatness. Lucky Luciano had a loose cannon in his organization by the name of Vito Genovese. Vito was in jail on a murder charge and the prosecutor had an eye witness. Vito was an original member of Lucky's crew and at one point was the acting boss of Luciano's crime family. Vito was a problem, but Lucky could not turn his back on a brother. Lucky arranged for the snitch to be taken out and Vito became a free man. I am not encouraging you to do anything illegal to help a friend, but I do want you to be aware of the potential dangers of your alliances so you can either disassociate yourself of help them prevent creating trouble for themselves as well as for you.

Deciding on a team is a two-way street. You may want to work with some individuals that may not want to work with you. It is always to your benefit to add value to every relationship. The value you add to the relationship is the collateral needed to forge long lasting alliances. Remember, tact is all about approach, your approach should always be appropriate for the persons you are recruiting to be a part of your team.

How do you find the right people? First you must become attractive to the marketplace, unforgettable, remember? Become larger than life. Do something meaningful. Reach out to people with similar goals. Help someone else achieve a task that is important to them. In some cases you will have to hire the right people to help you win. Ideally you want people that are down for the cause from day one. However, that is a rare breed of individuals and it is most likely that you will have to do things yourself and have some success before others will attach themselves to your cause. The most important thing you can do for yourself is to develop a trusted brand. **Proverbs 22:1** says, "Choose a good reputation over great riches; being held in high esteem is better than silver or gold."

Ultimately, your philosophy and mission will lead to your actions. You will measure your character against that which you believe. You will become who you are. And who you are will determine the impact you have on the world. Finally, that impact will not exist without the help of other like-minded individuals. Develop your tact, your approach, and strategically implement your tactics to get everything you want out of life.

RECAP

So far we have covered the "GET" of our journey. Moving forward we will get into the "IT." In the GET phase we have created a strong foundation and have begun working to get what we want. In the IT phase we will exam more tools to help us get IT. Now that we know our purpose and are sincere in our intentions, we are ready to develop our God given gifts and talents. We are ready to execute our plan with level headed tact. We are prepared to invest the necessary time needed to achieve our goal. We have learned from many successes and failures and are prepared to endure through our own peaks and valleys. The next two chapters will fully prepare us to begin our journey with full confidence that we can achieve the life we desire. GET excited! Pretty soon you will be dripping with awesome sauce. Let's talk about your intelligence.

Central Intelligence Agency
Play # 4 – Be Intelligent

A true sign of intelligence is not knowledge but imagination.
– Albert Einstein

The Central Intelligence Agency (CIA) is a civilian foreign intelligence service of the U.S. Government, tasked with gathering, processing and analyzing national security information from around the world, primarily through the use of human intelligence (HUMINT). At its core, the CIA's function is to study and counteract foreign threats to the United States of America. The Central Intelligence Agency has operatives all over the world, satellites, and strategists working tirelessly to neutralize threats and achieve the objectives set before them.

Becoming your own Central Intelligence Agent will help you to acquire the "knowledge of self" needed to excel in your purpose. Gathering information, processing, and analyzing it to capitalize on opportunities and to minimize risks and threats are skills that are often overlooked by individuals that fail to achieve their desired level of success. You will not fail! You will use your human intelligence, spiritual intelligence, and social intelligence to GET everything you want from life, because you are a Go Getter! So let's get it!

9/11

It was another beautiful morning in Atlanta, Georgia. I had training for my new job. Less health conscious than my older, wiser self, I stopped at McDonald's to get breakfast. The line was long and I was in a bit of hurry. Suddenly out of nowhere, I felt like I was dying. I could not breathe, my chest got really tight, and I thought I was having an Asthma attack. This feeling lasted for only a couple of minutes but it felt like a lifetime. The pain ran through my entire body. After it went away, I ordered my food and returned on my journey to work, baffled by what I'd just experienced.

Shortly after the training began, we were interrupted by the news of the Twin Towers. We turned on the news to see for ourselves. At the same exact time my body went into a panic, the first tower was hit. I'd had other instances where weird things had happened so this wasn't surprising to me. I was deeply saddened by this incident. 9/11 will never be forgotten by my generation as it marked the beginning of the War on Terrorism in the United States. It is not my function to argue conspiracies or theories, but only to illustrate my point as it applies to intelligence. Based on his propaganda, Osama Bin Laden, the head of al-Qaeda, an Islamist militant group, was the culprit and primary target for all of our operations.

Osama Bin Laden had successfully avoided capture for ten years before being killed in Pakistan on May 2, 2011 by Navy Seals in

Operation Neptune Spear, led by the CIA. Ten years of patience and gathering information led to the successful capture of Bin Laden. The CIA had Bin Laden's compound under surveillance for months before completing their mission. There were many "mini" missions that had to take place to acquire the needed intel to move in on "Public Enemy Number 1." After collecting what the government considered to be enough intel, they put Operation Neptune Spear into play. The Navy's mission was to kill or capture. Osama Bin Laden was killed. Mission accomplished.

You have a mission to accomplish. It may take three months; it might take ten years, but it is your duty to gather the information needed to accomplish the task and complete this mission. You cannot skip this step in life. You have to be willing to get your hands and knees dirty and scuffed up before the ride becomes smooth and easy. Patience is not a matter of waiting and doing nothing. It is the process of reaping the harvest from the investment of blood, sweat, and tears that you've made to design your life.

SWOT

College is a land of discovery. In college most students get their first taste of freedom and responsibility in a controlled environment. During my tenure at Michigan State University (Go Green, Go White), I began to dig deeper into knowing and understanding myself. Hip Hop during this era still had an element of consciousness. One of the leading voices was a group called Blackstar. Blackstar had a song called Knowledge of Self (Determination). Talib Kweli eloquently counteracts the stereotypes propagated by the more popular artists and the media. The song inspired me to look more closely at myself. I learned in one of my marketing classes how to do a SWOT Analysis. SWOT is an acronym for Strengths, Weaknesses, Opportunities, and Threats. Learning your purpose is the first step of becoming your own Central Intelligence Agency. However, knowing what you were created to do is not enough. You must examine yourself on a more intimate level. You need to understand your strengths and weaknesses. You need to know and take advantage of the opportunities in front of you. And like the CIA, you have to neutralize the threats preventing you from achieving your goals.

Strengths

What sets you apart from the crowd? What do you do better than everyone else? What advantages do you have, skills, certifications? These are questions that you have answered already in discovering your purpose. Knowing what you do best and doing it will make you happy and more fulfilled. As you examine your strengths, compare yourself to others around you. Make sure you are the One! If everyone around you is great at the same exact thing as you, then it is likely not your strength. For example, if you play basketball, and you shoot better than the other players on your team, that would be your strength. Another player may be better at passing the ball. Know and do what you do best.

Weaknesses

Our weaknesses are often easy to identify. Think about the things you avoid doing. What things in life do you feel less confident about or incompetent? What about personality traits that will make it difficult for you to compete? Recognizing our weaknesses is the first step to solidifying those areas in our lives. Whether that means improving personally, or by creating partnerships with others that are strong where we are weak to attain the desired results.

Opportunities

Opportunities are always among us. Often we have our eyes closed to them. Sometimes our strengths open doors of opportunity for us and weaknesses close doors. However, there are many things to examine like new technology, new trends and relationships. Recognizing a problem that needs to be solved and providing the solution is the greatest opportunity of them all. I remember hearing a talk about a gentleman that took on a project that no one in his office wanted to partake in. He excelled with the project and it resulted in a promotion and a substantial pay increase. Always remember, when there is a problem, there is an opportunity.

Threats

Threats are things that stand in the way of you and your goal. Some opportunities can also be threats. For example, technology could create an opportunity for you, but it can also replace the need for what you offer to the marketplace. Weaknesses can also lead to potential threats that you may not be prepared to face.

If you want to change the world, you must first change you. A personal SWOT analysis is a great way to dig more deeply into knowing yourself. It sounds funny, but a lot of people just do not know who they are. Some people know who they are but refuse to be honest about their disposition. Others know who they are and make no effort to improve or live up to their maximum potential. And a small minority are brutally honest with themselves and work their butts off to become great. Take a moment and reflect on which type of person described you relate to the most.

Mr. Personality

Swiss psychiatrist and psychotherapist, Carl Jung, was the founder of analytical psychology. Analytical psychology takes into account several big words, but as it relates to you, the Go Getter, it focuses on psychological types. Mr. Jung identified several attitudes and functions and considers consciousness as a factor leading to human behavior. Understanding your personality type may help you to narrow your path and focus on targeting and developing your strengths. This section will help you identify your personality and hopefully assist you growing into your gifts. Even scripture stresses the importance of self-examination. The Apostle Paul wrote in the book of Romans 12:3-8:

3 Because of the privilege and authority God has given me, I give each of you this warning: Don't think you are better than you really are. Be honest in your evaluation of yourselves, measuring yourselves by the faith God has given us. 4 Just as our bodies have many parts and each part has a special function, 5 so it is with Christ's body. We are many parts of one body, and we all belong to each other. 6 In his grace, God has given us different gifts for doing certain things well. So if God has given you the ability to prophesy, speak out with as much faith as God has given you. 7 If your gift is serving others, serve them well. If you are a teacher, teach well. 8 If your gift is to encourage others, be encouraging. If it is giving, give generously. If God has given you leadership ability, take the responsibility seriously. And if you have a gift for showing kindness to others, do it gladly.

Now let's examine the Attitudes and Functions of Mr. Jung's theory.

Attitudes
- **Introverted**
- **Extroverted**

Functions
- **Sensation** - perception by means of the sense organs;
- **Intuition** - perceiving in unconscious way or perception of unconscious contents.
- **Thinking** - function of intellectual cognition; the forming of logical conclusions;
- **Feeling** - function of subjective estimation;

The most popular extension of Jung's model is the Myer's Briggs Type Indicator. While Jung identified thirty-two personality types based on the combination of attitudes and functions, the Myer's Briggs Type Indicator narrows personality types down to sixteen types and adds a third element.

- **Judging** - organized and structured **or**
- **Perceiving**- free flowing and flexible

Judging and perceiving focuses on how a person uses the information he or she has processed. Putting this all together, we get **four** criteria for assessing the sixteen personality types.

Four Criteria for Personality Type Classification

1. Introversion (I) or Extraversion (E)

2. Sensing (S) or Intuition (N)
3. Thinking (T) or Feeling (F)
4. Judging (J) or Perceiving (P)

16 Personality Types

It is important to know that this information, while may be accurate, it is subjective. These personality type profiles can be found online in more detail at 16personalities.com. If you'd like a more in depth evaluation, I recommend taking their free personality test. Here's an overview of the 16 personality types.

INTJ

INTJ types are categorized as "Analysts." Considered an "Architect," INTJs have big imaginations and are strategic thinkers. INTJs are known to be knowledge seekers and have the drive to achieve their goals. This personality type has high standards and exudes confidence.

INTJs **strengths** are:

- Quick, Imaginative & Strategic Mind
- High Self Confidence
- Independent and Decisive
- Hardworking & Determined
- Open Minded
- Jack of All Trades

INTJs weaknesses include:
- Arrogance

- Judgmental
- Super Analytical
- Hate Highly Structured Environments

Mark Zuckerberg is a notable INTJ. Unlike myself, Mark was exposed to computers in middle school. By the time he was in high school he'd created games, communication tools, and various computer programs. One of those programs was a network that connected the computers of his home to his dad's dentistry practice. As a Harvard student, Zuckerberg was one of a few students that created Facebook. A genius of sorts, Zuckerberg has made Facebook one of the biggest phenomenon's of our lifetime.

The biggest risk is not taking any risk... In a world that's changing really quickly, the only strategy that is guaranteed to fail is not taking risks.
-Mark Zuckerberg

INTP

INTP types are categorized as "Analysts." Considered a "Logician," INTPs are known to be very logical and theoretical. INTPs are innovators, dreamers that can solve deep problems if they find an interest in something. This personality type is not very emotional and tends to have a fear of failure.

INTJs **strengths** are:

- Abstract Thinker
- Imaginative
- Open-Minded

- Enthusiastic
- Objective
- Honest & Straightforward

INTJs **weaknesses** include:

- Private & Withdrawn
- Insensitive
- Absent-Minded
- Condescending
- Hate Rules & Guidelines
- Second-Guess Themselves

Albert Einstein, the most world renowned physicist was considered an INTP. Einstein is credited with developing the general theory of relativity. $E=MC^2$ is his famous formula that was the result of his theory. Einstein was the most influential scientist of the 20th century. A Nobel Peace Prize winner, Einstein is the author of one of the most famous quotes of all time:

> *"Insanity is doing the same thing over and over*
> *again and expecting different results."*
> *-Albert Einstein*

ENTJ

ENTJ types are categorized as "Analysts." Considered a "Commander," ENTJs are bold and imaginative. ENTJs are frank, natural leaders that have a get it done kind of attitude. This personality type is very charismatic and confident and projects authority.

ENTJs **strengths** are:

- Efficient
- Energetic
- Self-Confident
- Strong-Willed
- Strategic Thinking
- Charismatic & Inspiring

ENTJs **weaknesses** include:

- Stubborn & Dominant
- Intolerant
- Impatient
- Arrogant
- Poor Handling of Emotions
- Cold & Ruthless

When Steve Jobs returned to Apple in 1997 after being ousted from the house he originally built, the company was in bad shape. There were multiple products being produced and there was a lack of focus. It is said that in a meeting, he pulled out the whiteboard, drew a grid that focused on four products and said all other products should be cancelled. Jobs was not one to rely on what the consumer thought, but believed in giving them what they wanted before they were aware that they wanted and needed it. Jobs was considered harsh, but a visionary that not only changed Apple, but changed the world with his concept of simplicity.

"Your work is going to fill a large part of your life, and the only way to be truly satisfied is to do what you believe is great work. And the only way to do great work is to love what you do. If you haven't found it yet, keep looking. Don't settle. As with all matters of the heart, you'll know when you find it."
–Steve Jobs

ENTP

ENTP types are categorized as "Analysts." Considered a "Debater," ENTPs are smart and curious. ENTPs like to play the "devil's advocate." This personality type is great at reading people and is resourceful at solving problems.

ENTPs **strengths** are:

- Knowledgeable
- Quick Thinkers
- Original
- Great at Brainstorming
- Charismatic
- Energetic

ENTPs **weaknesses** include:

- Very Argumentative
- Insensitive
- Intolerant
- Finds it Hard to Focus
- Dislikes Practical Matters

It takes a special type of individual to create something long lasting and impactful in this world. Walt Disney was such a person. Walt Disney's curiosity and ability to create an "experience" surpasses any other person in modern history. Who hasn't wanted to visit Disney World or watched a Disney movie? Walt Disney was definitely original and his criticisms were in line with his weaknesses. Some of the characters in Disney films could be offensive displaying his insensitivity but nonetheless, his creativity will be remembered for the ages.

You can dream, create, design and build the most wonderful place
in the world, but it requires people to make the dream a reality.
-Walt Disney

INFJ

INFJ types are categorized as "Diplomats." Considered an "Advocate," INFJs are quiet but inspiring. INFJs are the "helpers" of the world. This personality type has a "get it done" attitude and is willing to fight for what they believe in.

INFJs **strengths** are:

- Creative
- Inspiring and Convincing
- Decisive
- Determined and Passionate
- Altruistic

INFJs **weaknesses** include:

- Sensitive
- Extremely Private
- Perfectionist
- Always Need to Have a Cause
- Can Burn Out Easily

When your name is on street signs in every major city in the United States, it is safe to say that you may have inspired a nation. One of the most famous INFJs is Dr. Martin Luther King Jr. Dr. King had a dream that "one day right there in Alabama little black boys and little black girls will be able to join hands with little white boys and white girls as sisters and brothers." A great part of his dream has come to fruition. King believed, cared, inspired, and died to achieve his mission. I'd say he was a certified "Go Getter."

> *The ultimate measure of a man is not where he stands*
> *in moments of comfort and convenience, but where he*
> *stands at times of challenge and controversy.*
> *- Dr. Martin Luther King Jr.*

INFP

INFP types are categorized as "Diplomats." Considered a "Mediator," INFPs are thought to be reserved but are quietly passionate and poetic. INFPs are idealists that look for the good in every situation. This personality type can often be misunderstood because they are guided by principle rather than logic, but possess an uncanny ability for self-expression.

INFPs **strengths** are:

- Idealistic
- Seek and Value Harmony
- Open-Minded and Flexible
- Very Creative
- Passionate and Energetic
- Dedicated and Hardworking

INFPs **weaknesses** include:

- Too Idealistic
- Too Altruistic
- Impractical
- Dislike Dealing with Data
- Take Things Personally
- Difficult to Get to Know

Several famous writers that have influenced society are INFPs. Shakespeare (Hamlet, Macbeth, Romeo and Juliet) is pretty much required reading in universities worldwide. J.R.R. Tolkien (The Lord of the Rings) and J.K. Rowling (Harry Potter) have seen their books become big screen phenomena as well as C.S. Lewis' "The Chronicles of Narnia." All of these books and movies require creativity, open-mindedness and an idealistic mindset.

God cannot give us a happiness and peace apart from
Himself, because it is not there. There is no such thing.
– C.S. Lewis

ENFJ

ENFJ types are categorized as "Diplomats." Considered a "Protagonist," ENFJs are natural born leaders. ENFJs are usually the coaches and teachers of the world. ENFJs have a genuine concern for the people.

ENFJs **strengths** are:

- Tolerant
- Reliable
- Charismatic
- Altruistic
- Natural Leaders

ENFJs **weaknesses** include:

- Overly Idealistic
- Too Selfish
- Too Sensitive
- Fluctuating Self-Esteem
- Struggle to Make Tough Decisions

The most monumental of all ENFJs is President Barack Obama. In a system designed to exclude African Americans, President Obama rose through the ranks to become the country's leader and first African American president serving two terms in office. Very charismatic, Obama is considered the people's President because of his use of social influence and technology to campaign and to get elected. And some may argue that during his tenure that the country improved fiscally. Obama is definitely a natural born leader, more tolerant (not sure if this is good or bad) than most, and he definitely is idealistic (Obamacare???).

> *If you're walking down the right path and you're willing*
> *to keep walking, eventually you'll make progress.*
> *– Barack Obama*

ENFP

ENFP types are categorized as "Diplomats." Considered a "Campaigner," ENFPs are enthusiastic and free-spirited. ENFPs are idealists that look for the good in every situation. This personality type can often be misunderstood because they are guided by principle rather than logic, but possess an uncanny ability for self-expression.

ENFPs **strengths** are:

- Curious
- Observant
- Energetic and Enthusiastic

- Excellent Communicators
- Know How to Relax
- Very Popular & Friendly

ENFPs **weaknesses** include:

- Poor Practical Skills

- Find it Hard to Focus
- Over Thinks Things
- Gets Stressed Easily
- Highly Emotional
- Independent to a Fault

Depending on who you ask, Ché Guevara is either a hero or a tyrant. Whatever he was, his image on T-Shirts worn by Americans worldwide proves that he was significant. Guevara is a symbol of revolution demonstrating how popular an ENFP can be.

If you tremble with indignation at every injustice,
then you are a comrade of mine.
– Ché Guevara

ISTJ

ISTJ types are categorized as "Sentinels." Considered a "Logistician," ISTJs are practical and exhibit exceptional character. ISTJs are dedicated and take pride in their work and duties.

ISTJs **strengths** are:

- Honest and Direct
- Strong-willed and Dutiful
- Very Responsible
- Calm and Practical
- Create and Enforce Order
- Jacks-of-All-Trades

ISTJs **weaknesses** include:

- Stubborn
- Insensitive
- Always by the Book
- Judgmental
- Often Unreasonably Blame Themselves

There are four companies that pretty much have a monopoly as it relates to technology in this present age: Google, Apple, Facebook, and Amazon. Jeff Bezos, founder of Amazon was born to a teenage mom, graduated from Princeton, worked on Wall Street, and quit his lucrative job as the youngest Senior Vice President at investment firm D.E. Shaw to open Amazon.com. Bezos is passionate about creating a great customer experience. Under his leadership Amazon has become the leader in online e-commerce.

> *Your brand is what other people say about*
> *you when you are not in the room.*
> *– Jeff Bezos*

ISFJ

ISFJ types are categorized as "Sentinels." Considered a "Defender," ISFJs are the service oriented personality type. Though introverted, they have great social skills. Though they are led more by feeling, they have the ability to be analytical as well. ISFJs are likely to be our doctors, teachers, military, and anyone dedicated to service.

ISFJs **strengths** are:

- Supportive
- Reliable and Patient
- Imaginative and Observant
- Enthusiastic
- Loyal & Hardworking
- Good Practical Skills

ISFJs **weaknesses** include:

- Humble & Shy
- Take Things Too Personally
- Repress Their Feelings
- Overload Themselves
- Reluctant to Change
- Too Altruistic

Without a doubt in mind, Kanye West is one of the more entertaining ISFJs. An imaginative, patient, hard worker, Kanye will definitely go down in history for his music and social commentary. As reflective in his music, Kanye is an emotional fellow. Often quiet but boisterous at the same time, Kanye exhibits the characteristics of an ISFJ via his artistic endeavors.

My Music isn't just music– it's medicine!
- Kanye West

I would be remiss not to mention one other ISFJ that embodied all that is good in the world, Mrs. Rosa Parks. Rosa Parks' single act of bravery helped to ignite a oneness of the people that led to a dramatic and revolutionary time in American history. If Aretha Franklin will forever be immortalized as the Queen of Soul, Rosa Parks will forever be the Mother of Civil Rights.

> *"The advice I would give any young person is ... to be concerned about what they can do to help others."*
> –Rosa Parks

ESTJ

ESTJ types are categorized as "Sentinels." Considered an "Executive," ESTJs are excellent administrators with a knack for managing people and resources. This personality type is all about leading by example and working hard to build character.

ESTJs **strengths** are:

- Dedicated
- Strong-willed
- Direct and Honest
- Loyal, Patient and Reliable
- Enjoy Creating Order
- Excellent Organizers

ESTJs **weaknesses** include:

- Inflexible and Stubborn
- Uncomfortable with Unconventional Situations
- Judgmental
- Too Focused on Social Status
- Difficult to Relax

- Difficulty Expressing Emotion

One of my favorite ladies in the world is First Lady Michelle Obama. Guys want a girl like her and the ladies want to be her. Michelle Obama exhibits elegance and grace. A Princeton and Harvard Law School grad, the first African American First lady, Mrs. Obama is a role model and inspiration to many.

> *Role modeling what good families should look like [is important]. And my view is that if you can't run your own house, you certainly can't run the White House.*
> *– Michelle Obama*

ESFJ

ESFJ types are categorized as "Sentinels." Considered a "Consul," ESFJs are socialites by nature. Usually popular, or representative of the "in crowd," ESFJs are known to lead their teams to victory. ESFJs **strengths** are:

- Strong Practical Skills
- Strong Sense of Duty
- Very Loyal
- Sensitive and Warm
- Good at Connecting with Others

ESFJs **weaknesses** include:

- Worried About Social Status
- Inflexible

- Reluctant to Innovate and Improvise
- Vulnerable to Criticism
- Often Too Needy
- Too Selfless

Andrew Carnegie was the pioneer of steel. Responsible for the expansion of the steel industry in America, Carnegie made his fortune as an industrialist and was a known philanthropist, giving away more than $5 billion dollars in today's figures to charitable causes and foundations.

People who are unable to motivate themselves must be content with mediocrity, no matter how impressive their other talents.
-Andrew Carnegie

ISTP

ISTP types are categorized as "Explorers." Considered a "Virtuoso," ISTPs are the "makers" of the world. ISTPs are likely to reverse engineer things. They love to put things together and take them apart to see how they work.

ISTPs **strengths** are:

- Optimistic & Energetic
- Creative and Practical
- Spontaneous and Rational
- Know How to Prioritize
- Great in a Crisis
- Relaxed

ISTPs **weaknesses** include:

- Stubborn
- Insensitive
- Private and Reserved
- Easily Bored
- Dislike Commitment
- Risky Behavior

A beloved martial artist, philosopher, and filmmaker, Bruce Lee exhibits the best use of the ISTPs strengths. Lee's unique brand of Kung Fu and on screen personality elevated Lee to an iconic level.

The key to immortality is first living a life worth remembering.
-Bruce Lee

Use only that which works, and take it from any place you can find it.
-Bruce Lee

ISFP

ISFP types are categorized as "Explorers." Considered an "Adventurer," ISFPs are the true "artist" type. Spontaneous and unpredictable accurately describes this type.

ISFPs **strengths** are:

- Charming
- Sensitive to Others
- Imaginative

- Passionate
- Curious
- Artistic

ISFPs **weaknesses** include:

- Fiercely Independent
- Unpredictable
- Easily Stressed
- Overly Competitive
- Fluctuating Self Esteem

Two gentleman that exude artistry and have had a tremendous impact on the world through music are Michael Jackson and Prince. Musically, there are only a few geniuses whose compositions stand the test of time and MJ and Prince are in that elite company. Both artists embody all of the strengths and weaknesses of the ISFP and have documented these traits in the music they've created.

The meaning of life is contained in every single
expression of life. It is present in the infinity of forms
and phenomena that exist in all of creation.
–Michael Jackson

The key to longevity is to learn every aspect of music that you can.
– Prince

ESTP

ESTP types are categorized as "Explorers." Considered an "Entrepreneur," ESTPs enjoy being the center of attention. ESTPs are likely to be the riskiest of all personality traits. Doing and learning as they go, ESTPs feel like rules are meant to be broken and will do so.

ESTPs **strengths** are:

- Bold
- Rational and Practical
- Original
- Perceptive
- Direct
- Sociable

ESTPs **weaknesses** include:

- Insensitive
- Impatient
- Risk-prone
- Unstructured
- May Miss the Bigger Picture
- Defiant

Two ESTPs that have influenced my life via their writings are el-Hajj Malik el-Shabazz and Dale Carnegie. Both men overcame poverty to influence the world for decades to come. The **Autobiography of Malcolm X** was heralded by the New York Times as a brilliant, painful, and important book. Dale Carnegie's book, **How to**

Win Friends and Influence People is a staple in every successful entrepreneur or business person's library.

Any time you find someone more successful than you are ...
you know they're doing something that you aren't.
–Malcolm X

Success is getting what you want. Happiness is wanting what you get.
–Dale Carnegie

ESFP

ESFP types are categorized as "Explorers." Considered an "Entertainer," ESFPs love the spotlight. Super social creatures, ESFPs tend to be among the famous in society and are always willing to share of themselves with the world.

ESFPs **strengths** are:

- Bold
- Original
- Aesthetics and Showmanship
- Practical
- Observant
- Excellent People Skills

ESFPs **weaknesses** include:

- Sensitive
- Conflict-Averse

- Easily Bored
- Poor Long-Term Planners
- Unfocused

Will Smith and Denzel Washington transcend success and mastery of their craft. There are few actors that become the character they are playing. Consummate showmen, both men are bold enough to play tough roles, original enough to own them, and pay attention to the details of the art.

I say luck is when an opportunity comes along and you're prepared for it.
- Denzel Washington

In my mind, I've always been an A-list Hollywood superstar. Y'all just didn't know yet.
-Will Smith

While personality testing can provide insight on your life, it is not the end all, be all. You may exhibit strengths and weaknesses of various personality types. The purpose of learning this information is to help you get on the right track of self-discovery.

The Brand Man

Hajj Flemings is someone I consider a mentor and friend. Hajj is an author and the founder of Brand Camp University, I've watched Hajj grow his brand from a book, to continued Fortune 100 sponsorships from companies like Google and IBM for his Brand Camp events. Over the years, I have been inspired by Hajj's message, but more by his example. One thing Hajj taught me when I began my personal branding journey was the importance of a mission statement. When you know who you are, and identify what you want and are meant to accomplish in the world, a personal mission statement will help you maintain your focus as you move forward throughout life. When you face adversities or self-doubt, this statement is what you can read to remind yourself of your "why."

As humans, we have the freedom to do as we please. And as Jeff Bezos is quoted as saying, "Your brand is what people say when you are not in the room." It is important for you to have a brand intelligence. You must be cognizant of the story and message that you project with everything from the way you speak, to the way you dress, to even your posture. Position yourself for success, and it will not feel like luck when you attain it. In the world of intelligence, managing your reputation by being known for your integrity and character will carry you a long way as you journey to your idea of success. CONTROL YOUR BRAND.

Your Gift Will Make a Way

My biological father and I have an estranged relationship that exists because of a promise I made to my grandfather. The last time I saw my grandfather alive he called me to come talk. This was slightly unusual as I normally just went to check on him when I was in town. When I sat down with my grandfather he said to me, "Ron Ron, I want you to forgive your father." Being that my grandfather had never sat me down and had a heart to heart conversation with me before, I knew this was a serious matter. I respected my grandfather and promised that I would do my best.

Forgiving my father was a difficult task. Our relationship started on the wrong foot. As the story goes, my dad was a drug addict, that at some point beat on my mom and stole the money she'd saved up to take care of me when I was born to feed his addiction. Memories of my dad as a young child were far and few in between. Some of the ones I have were good, but along with those good memories, were the ones where I asked my mom, "When is he coming?" "Why doesn't he love me?" Honestly, I did not know the full truth about my dad until I was able to live with him for a summer. I don't remember the altercation between he and my stepmom, but I do remember his fist going through the wall. I do remember my baseball glove mysteriously disappearing. None the less, I loved my dad.

Things changed for me as a teenager. I'd say me and my father were on pretty good terms throughout my high school years. He seemed pretty stable then. But the storm was brewing and I had no idea or clue as to what type of person he really was until I started college. He gave me a credit card to buy books. When I tried to use the card it was declined. During that year, I also found out that my dad was severely ill with a drug addiction and was stealing money from my grandmother. That was the straw that broke the camel's back for me. My grandmother was a saint in my eyes (though her past was pretty gangster) and I became enraged with hate towards my father.

When I graduated from college, he'd chosen a church event to attend instead of my graduation, but showed up for my dinner celebration with a card in his hand. "Son, I got you something!" I was happy. My mother was furious that he did not attend the graduation, but I wasn't tripping because this was normal behavior and I was happy that he had gotten clean. Disappointment did not settle in until I opened the card and it was from my grandfather, not my dad. Needless to say, forgiving my father would be one of the hardest things I would do in my life, but I was determined to do so in honor of my granddad.

All of my life I heard stories about how smart my dad was. School was easy for him. Charisma, he had that and a mouthpiece to get in and out of almost any situation. Ronald Sr. was quick on his toes and slick as a can of oil. He wanted to be a musician. He played the clarinet and was friends with Ray Parker Jr., who was famous for writing the Ghostbusters' theme song. According to my father, my grandfather thought music was a joke and that he should go to college for business. I believe he went for one semester and dropped out. My father didn't follow his passion. I am not sure exactly when my father veered off onto the dark side but eventually he did. Most of my experiences with him were in relation to that season of his life. Though he did not use his gifts, follow his dreams, or purpose, he would drop a few jewels on me every now and then that I've kept close to my chest. One thing he taught me that I remember and strived to implement in my life is:

Learn from my mistakes. You don't have to put your hand on the eye of the stove to know that it is hot. If you see someone else get burned, that should be enough to help you avoid the same fate.

Experience is the most respected form of intelligence. All experiences do not have to be hands on for you to gather wisdom and applicable knowledge. Learning from my father's mistakes meant that I would not ignore my gifts and instincts. Despite believing that I was extremely different from my father, I learned that I wasn't. For years I despised my gifts and allowed them to lay dormant. Mostly because I was unaware of what I had to offer the world. I have always been the person others have come to for advice. As a younger person, I hated it. I had my own problems, but everyone I knew wanted me to solve theirs. I was known to be a straight shooter. No holds barred, tell-you-like-it-is type of person. To the sensitive person, I was mean, but the truth is that I lacked tact.

I was always a little different, a little more creative, more imaginative, and oddly enough, more observant than most young people. I enjoyed sitting amongst the elders and soaking up wisdom, game, and anything else I thought I'd be able to use to help me navigate through life. Some would say, "You've been here before." or "You have an old soul." I just thought I didn't have time for nonsense and didn't want to hear what you were talking about if it didn't further my cause. I admit, I was a little selfish.

Post marriage, a few kids, a lot of new experiences, and an open ear to God, I have come to embrace the opportunity to guide people in the right direction. I won't lie, I have run from this moment for many years. The responsibility of the lives of others is a big one that I'm not eager to drop the ball on. As I have begun to embrace my purpose, I have noticed many opportunities come my way. The more I do what I am purposed to do, the more I use my gift, the more fulfilling my life becomes. Even in tough seasons, when most people would quit, I find hope in my work because I know that I am doing what I am supposed to do. I know I am using my gifts and talents to do what I was created to do.

I want to encourage you to use your talents, develop your strengths and apply them to the service of making life better for those around you. Understanding your strengths and developing them is a form of intelligence that my father missed out on, that I almost destroyed, and a mistake that many make today. Do not feed your mind doubt. Don't feed your mind fear. Feed your spirit things that will help you to advance. Our society today is so media driven that our views, thoughts, and feelings are spoon fed to us and programmed into our psyche. Developing your gift, so that it can make a way for you requires you to turn the television off. It requires you to not hang out with your friends every weekend. You may have to minimize your exposure to certain relationships. Here is a quote by Steve Siebold from **How Rich People Think:**

> *Walk into a wealthy person's home and one of the first thing*
> *you'll see is an extensive library of books they've used to*
> *educate themselves on how to become more successful.*

Allowing your gift to make a way for you is the best way to ensure success. Educate yourself, about yourself, and become who you are meant to be. My wife is an educator, a great educator in fact. The one thing that she stresses is this: It is not how smart you are; it is *how* you are smart. You are the CIA, begin your covert operation: Know Thyself.

> *It is not how smart you are; it is how you are smart.*
> *-Mari Elliott*

Imagination

Easily the rarest form of intelligence, imagination is an underutilized or overly scrutinized tool. Every Go Getter should spend time developing this gift. Fortunately, this is something we all have and actually possess the power to control. Once you master your individual gifts and talents, mixing a little imagination can help you to create magical life moments. The world's greatest inventions and devices began with a "What if?" Imagination is often shot down by the shortsighted. If you have limited vision you will travel a limited distance.

Orville and Wilbur Wright are credited for creating the first airplane. However, they were not the first. What they did accomplish was the creation of the first aircraft with controls that would allow a pilot to navigate the friendly skies. Their vision to provide a way to travel via air rather than by ground and water has revolutionized the way we view travel. Now there are people making down payments on a flight to the moon. Imagine what type of jokes the Wright brothers must have endured when they told someone we are going to fly with the birds. They likely heard things like, "You guys are crazy!" or "It can't be done!" or "Why waste your time?" However, their imaginations allowed them to be free from their limitations. Never be afraid to dream. Never fear making your dreams a reality. Exercise your creativity every chance you get. Your imagination has limitless possibilities.

Pure Imagination

Come with me, and you'll be
In a world of Pure Imagination
Take a look, and you'll see
Into your imagination
We'll begin with a spin
Traveling in the world of my creation.

What we'll see will defy explanation
If you want to view paradise
Simply look around and view it. Anything you want to, do it
Want to change the world?
There's nothing to it
There is no life I know
To compare with Pure Imagination
Living there you'll be free
If you truly wish to be
If you want to view paradise
Simply look around and view it
Anything you want to, do it
There is no life like I know
To compare with Pure Imagination
Living there you'll be free
If you truly wish to be
(From the Movie- Willy Wonka & The Chocolate Factory)

Time After Time
Play # 5 – Value Time

A budget is telling your money where to go
instead of wondering where it went.
–Dave Ramsey

Dave Ramsey helps millions of people get out of debt and build stable financial situations via his books, seminars, radio, and television programs. One principal Dave teaches is the "Debt Snowball." A debt snowball is when you put all of your additional income towards a debt monthly until the debt is paid. Once that particular debt is paid, you apply the funds that you have freed, plus the additional income you began with to another debt. This method helps you to rid yourself of the total debt in a shorter amount of time than simply paying the minimum amounts due.

Once you are out of debt, Dave is big on funding your retirement. If you are a financially educated young person, you have a huge advantage on the rest of society. Investing in the market at a young age dramatically increases your chances of accumulating millions of dollars before you reach retirement age. Even if you do not begin saving for retirement until the age of forty, you can amass a million dollars if you apply the right amount of your monthly income to the right interest bearing accounts over a twenty year period. However, the amount of investment and the time frame differs greatly between the young and the old. The young can create a million dollar fund with $20,000 or less over a ten year period versus the $200,000 or more it takes the forty year old. The difference maker is TIME.

Habitually Speaking

The **7 Habits of Highly Effective People** is a staple book for anyone looking to improve productivity. At the core of his teaching, Stephen Covey focuses on developing character; taking an inside-out approach to achieving success. In taking this approach, Covey guides the reader through three stages: Dependence, Independence, and Interdependence. The idea is to move from lacking the character it takes, to being highly effective and transitioning to a place where one can work cohesively with a team to achieve success. In other words, if you have to depend on people to survive, you are incapable of being effective. If you are independent, you will soon learn that success is a team sport. And if you become interdependent, a master of your craft and partner with other masters of their own crafts to create winning situations, you will be more likely to succeed.

The first three of the Seven Habits are:
1. Be Proactive
2. Begin with the End in Mind
3. Put First Things First

These three habits are critical to the idea of maximizing your time.

Be Proactive

The first, being proactive means making a decision to change. Proactivity requires you to apply yourself to something and not allow life to happen you. There is an old saying, "Nothing comes to a dreamer but a dream." In terms of Hip Hop, OutKast and Goodie Mob said it best, "You need to git up, git out, and git somethin..." The concept here is that you will either act, or be acted upon.

Begin with the End in Mind

Earlier in the book I mentioned how I learned to have a personal mission statement from one of my mentors, Hajj Flemings. Beginning with the end in mind means focusing your efforts only on things that will help you achieve that mission. If something does not align with your principles, it should not be present in your goals.

Put First Things First

Prioritize your purpose and mission. Do the things that are most important to achieving your goals first. Life is more complex than just doing what you want to do, we have families, jobs, and all the responsibilities that come with those areas of life. It is easy to become distracted, so it is important to schedule the activities that align with your purpose first.

The Construct of Time

Some people believe time does not really exist, that time is simply a man-made theory. While we have assigned a numerical system to measure time, the truth is what we refer to as "Time" does elapse. Whether it is a social construct or not, we are a social creation therefore valuing the time you have on earth is essential. Our social construct has deceived many into believing the theory of Time being equal to Money. While it sounds good, it is very untrue. Mostly because of two factors. The first factor is that Time is a continuum. When Time passes, it is gone, never to be recaptured. Yesterday stays in the past. Moments exists like brief winds. Money on the other hand can be gained, lost, and regained. The second factor is that earning money does not have to be linked with time. Some people make money in their sleep, while others labor tirelessly exchanging most of their waking hours to earn a livable wage.

Time is to be valued above virtually all that we have stewardship over. "Time Management" is a huge buzzword amongst the successful. However, how do you manage something that you cannot control? A better way to view time is by Time Maximization or making the most of the time you have. We are often limited in our accomplishments by the way we prioritize our time. It is common to hear people say, "I would do… but I do not have enough time!" The truth is most people have not identified their purpose and begun the passionate pursuit of fulfilling it. Most people put last things first. It is easy to procrastinate and not be proactive about the things we really want. After all, everything we really want, takes work and dedication. Achieving our goals requires diligence and patience throughout the process of attainment.

There are twenty-four hours in a day and as long as we've been awarded the chance to open our eyes and get out of the bed, we all have the same amount of time to accomplish what is important. Those that master how they use the allotted time given to them live the life most desire. The goal is to master oneself. Therefore the focus should not be "Time Management" but self-management. At the end of the day the only thing one really has control of is him/herself.

Bruce Lee is to martial arts what Michael Jackson is to pop music, or Michael Jordan to basketball. Bruce Lee was a master of the art he taught and demonstrated a level of supremacy that was unmatched. Bruce Lee once said, "I fear not the man who has practiced 10,000 kicks once, but I fear the man who has practiced one kick 10,000 times." In other words, the person that focuses on one thing, is more dangerous than the person that focuses on many. Lack of purpose, ambition, and/or despair can send a person scrambling, practicing 10,000 kicks once. I understand it, I've been there, done that. I've tried many things to get ahead. I've started many businesses. I've acquired many skills. Education, did that. Worked a 100 jobs too. That way of living got me nowhere.

However, it was not until I truly learned the importance of prioritizing my purpose did I begin to feel accomplished. Now I am practicing the same kick every moment possible. What is your "kick?" What is your one thing? Are you prioritizing and maximizing your time to focus on mastery? Remember the story of Warren Buffett and selecting the five most important things. When you have done this, life really begins and everything else becomes a faint memory of failure.

Four Quarters

In organized basketball, aside from the NCAA, the game is played in four quarter increments. While the ultimate goal is to win the game, the strategy and tactics implemented to win are adjusted during each quarter. Most coaches focus on winning the quarters. The team that wins the most quarters, wins the game. During my process of mastering personal development, I've encountered people and resources to help me along the way. One such person is a former basketball teammate.

Aaron and I played high school ball together. I am not sure how we linked back up in our adulthood, but since it has occurred, Aaron has been someone that has cheered me on and provided good consul. Remember, success is a team sport. One thing that Aaron and I have in common is our desire to help people achieve personal greatness. Aaron does this as a youth minister and corporate trainer. A few years back, Aaron noticed that I was doing too much. He gave me a book that changed the way I looked at my priorities forever. I'd already spent some time studying effectiveness and productivity. In fact, I was a master of multitasking. However, while I was doing a lot, I was not doing enough of the right thing to get the right result. I'd see glimpses of success, because honestly, I wasn't giving one thing all of my attention. The book Aaron gave me was called the **12 Week Year**. In it was a simple concept: Pick one project that you want to complete and schedule the needed time and resources to get it done within 12 weeks. I always had a hundred things that I wanted to get done. Reading that book made me think more deeply about my mission and what I really wanted to accomplish. And like most people, I read it, but I did not apply it immediately. That is a huge mistake.

When we learn new things, it is in our best interest to test them immediately. The sooner we test them, the sooner we know if they work, and if they do, the sooner we get results. Playing the game of life quarterly is a great way to ensure that you are working on your top five. Imagine what your 12 month year could look like if you accomplished four major goals within it!

VIP

In my late twenties I attended and graduated from Bible school. This was a very exciting time for me in life because I was growing in my knowledge and my personal relationship with God at an astronomical rate. I was hungry and thirsty to learn more about the Creator. I was one of those people that was surely going to have a VIP suite in Hell before I experienced the love of the Messiah. My path of destructive behavior was long and even worse, mostly without punishment or repercussion. I was definitely my father's child except my addiction wasn't a drug. God's love changed me, and that love led me to want to know more, and be worthy of the salvation awarded to me.

During my time of enlightenment, I was fortunate to have a pastor that was well organized and sharp. As a student at the school, I was privy to some resources that others may not have known about. One of those was an organization for the ministers in the church. I was able to get my hands on some of the teachings specific to this organization. One of the teachings was about Priorities. The lesson taught a system called VIP. "V" represented the very important things that you must accomplish in your daily life. "I" represented the "Important" things and "P" is for the productive things that we must accomplish.

Additionally, if I recall, it taught about prioritizing our lives into compartments: God, Self, Family, Business, Ministry.

As I continued my path to personal mastery (still on the journey) I began to combine what I'd learned from church with the 7 Habits, and the 12 Week Year. I also do something similar to the Warren Buffett method, though it is on a smaller scale. Finding a system to organize your life will make it much more simple. You will find that you have more than enough time to do the things you desire if you take the time to prioritize every area of life. Just like with your money, every dollar should have a purpose, every hour of your day should have a purpose. The person that creates a plan and does all they can to stick to it, is the person that is quickest to achieve personal success.

Timing is Everything

Most successful people do not believe in luck. Why? Because for those that master themselves, luck is something you create for yourself through preparation. If you are prepared when opportunity strikes, you improve your chances to capitalize on the opportunity. The key to having impeccable timing is to be prepared and always looking for the opportunity. Think back to your personal SWOT Analysis. What things do you observe in your world can you improve upon and make your mark? You can have a brilliant idea, but if you are not prepared to share it when the time is right, it can quickly become an early morning mist that disappears when the sun awakes.

My good friend John always says, "Money answers all things… follow the money." John is an investor. He does well observing the trends in the world and in the market. We often bet each other for breakfast on sporting outcomes and most times I lose. Knowing the trends, where the money is moving, will help you know when it is the right time to move on something. Do not hesitate. If you have taken the time to read this book and apply the major concepts of the five plays, the five steps, you should be prepared. Now it is time to capture your opportunity.

In The Moment

Small children have no idea about the concept of time. There is no past, no future, only the present time. They live for the moment, expecting to receive everything they cry out to possess. When I walk in the door from a long day of work, I am greeted by four little girls screaming "Daddy!!!" while my legs and hands are quickly accosted. The brightness in their eyes and the joy in their voice give me a feeling that I wish I could bottle and sell. In that moment, I am reminded of what we are all in pursuit of, happiness.

When was the last time you took a moment to take it all in? We are often reliving our glory days or past struggles. If not recounting the past, we fantasize about our glorious future. Reminiscing about the past is useless, unless you are looking for lessons to help you in the present. Dwelling on the past can be detrimental. Thinking on it, when faced with a current problem is good, however, the primary focus should be the present. When you speak too much on your glory days subconsciously you are saying you are not happy with your life as it "is." Stay in the moment and you will remain driven to fulfill your purpose. If your glory days are a constant subject for you, ask yourself what about that time made you happy? What did you appreciate about the moment? Then in the Now, do the things that make your glory days your present.

Being too focused on the future can prevent you from becoming the best you, as well. For some, tomorrow brings new worries and concerns. For others, the future is a way to avoid the realities of today. Thinking about tomorrow too much is, simply put, a distraction. Having goals and dreams are great and very important, but if you spend all your time dreaming and no time doing, your dream will remain a dream.

Despite past pains or victories and big dreams or plans, those that really GET what they want out of life turn their attention to the Now. So enjoy the journey. Let go of yesterday and let tomorrow care for itself. When you laugh, laugh hard. When you have the opportunity to stand in the sun, appreciate the greatness of it and its purpose. Listen to the birds chirp or the waves of the water. What good is it to be in a high speed chase to success if you don't roll down the windows or drop the top and feel the wind blowing in your face? The point is, do not obsess over your past or future, nor become a slave to your current circumstance. Grieve your pains the day they happen and forget them the next day. Celebrate your victories when they happen but show up to practice the next day ready to work again. Plan ahead for the future but start working the plan Now!

The Little Foxes

> *15 Catch all the foxes, those little foxes, before they ruin the vineyard of love, for the grapevines are blossoming!*
> *–Solomon 2:15 (NLT)*

Your vineyard may not be love, but your dreams are ripe and ready to come to fruition. And there are many little foxes in your life ready to ruin your success. These foxes are the time wasters that get in the way of our daily tasks preventing us from maximizing our time. Here is a list of the Top 4 Time Wasting Activities:

1. **Social Media**- Social media seems ubiquitous in our society. It is on our phones, computers, tablets, TVs, and even our watches! Think about how often you check your phone to see a stat, pic, or video. Most likely those little minutes can add up to at least an hour of productive activity. I encourage you to try to eliminate social media from your life for the next 48 hours and do something productive every time you get the urge to use social media.

2. **Television**- Television is likely the biggest time waster of all-time. It is not uncommon for most households to have a television in every room. The average American watches five or more hours of television every day. If you are the average American that is about thirty hours per week. Imagine what you could accomplish in a year if you cut that number in half. Take it a step further, what if you got down to an hour a day! Cut out television and really maximize your time.

3. **Exercise**- This almost feels sacrilegious writing considering that I've been a health and fitness professional for over 10 years, but it is true. During my tenure as personal trainer, I'd always tell my clients to work smart and hard for thirty to forty-five minutes every day and go enjoy life. If fitness is your profession that's different. If fitness is not your profession,

spend a little less time in the gym and improve your eating habits so that you can remain healthy and not waste time being sick.

4. **Not Saying No-** Helping others is a great thing. However, if you spend more time building other people's kingdoms than you do yours, you will never have the life you truly want. I had to learn how to say no other's visions and yes to mine. The more smaller jobs you sign up to do, the less time you have to focus on the MAIN THING.

Stick To The Script-The Main Thing

During my time in the network marketing industry I had the pleasure of discovering many great teachers. One of those teachers was Mark, the World's Laziest Networker. Mark was a great teacher because his methods were always simple, quick, and effective. One thing Mark really helped me with was keeping the "Main Thing," the "Main Thing."

Similar to Warren Buffett's rule of five, keeping the main thing, the main thing is a matter of only doing what you do best. Anything, and I mean anything you can outsource, you should. In my VIP system, the goal is to occupy my time with (Very Important) matters. Some (Important) things are unavoidable, but the (Productive) issues at hand, I try to delegate elsewhere. The same hour of time it may take me to clean my house could be used to shoot a motivational video or write a speech.

The Main Thing is what we were made to do. It is what we do effortlessly, yet most of us neglect what makes us awesome. It is imperative that we stick to the script. Improvising our way through life will yield various results. Finding our purpose and living it will lead you to the promise land.

Improvisation is a great skill to possess and comes in handy when life throws us curveballs. However, shooting off of the hip is never as accurate as aiming with a laser sighting. Maximizing your time is all about focus. Focus only on what is important. Treat everything else like Sideshow Bob. You may have to address these things for a few episodes of life but you cannot afford to make your distractions the Main characters of your life.

The Value Add

The valuation of your time should be assessed on a regular basis. We often allow others to determine our value rather than setting our own value. I live for helping people become who they are intended to become. I have a special affinity for young people. I work with youth on a regular basis, most of the work is compensated, some is my personal contribution to my community. I have a contract with a local non-profit, The Yunion to deliver their Abstinence curriculum. This is a really great organization with a heart for families and youth. If you are looking for an organization to contribute to where the work is definitely getting done, I encourage you to visit their website: http://theyunion.org.

Though I am paid for my service, I'd be willing to do the work I do with the Yunion for free. When I started my journey as a speaker, this organization provided me with one of my first opportunities. I am compensated well for the work I do with this program. However, when I decided to step out fully by faith, I was able to charge 10x as much for the same amount of time rendered. Obviously, a non-profit cannot afford to pay my standard fee for the frequency in which I work, but if I did not value my personal time to be worth 10x more, I would have played myself by charging what I get paid to work with the Yunion.

You can demand more if you add more value to those you serve. Think back to your SWOT Analysis. What problem does your strengths help you solve? People are willing to pay whatever is necessary to solve their problems. It is imperative that we invest time in becoming "value adding" individuals.

Personal Development

Personal development is essential to becoming a "value adding" individual. Most successful people spend time early in the morning tending to their personal wellbeing. Some pray, others meditate. They exercise their spirits, minds, and bodies. Setting a dedicated time for your personal growth is essential to your success. In addition to setting a time, you must create a plan for how you will use it. Rome was not built in a day and neither will your life be.

The time you are dedicating to reading this book already proves that you are committed to your personal growth. There are two approaches to personal development in regards to reading. Some believe you should read as many books as you can each year and others believe you should master the principles of one before moving on to the next. I am a more-free flowing type of guy so to be honest, I haven't used either of these techniques in a manner to suggest which is best. I encourage you to pick the method that is most attractive to you and try it.

Personal development from the standpoint of health and fitness is essential because we need our bodies to function properly if we want to be world changers, right? The best way to motivate others is to first motivate yourself. Your life as you live it is a testimony to others. As a Certified Personal Trainer I have learned this lesson first hand. I took job at a gym once where the previous trainer was not too enthusiastic about his job. Upon my arrival, the number of training sessions skyrocketed. Each new person stated that they never wanted to sign up for training because the other trainer did not seem to care. This particular gym paid an hourly wage, so we got paid whether we were with a client or not. However, we were required to execute a certain amount of sessions per week. By my second month at this gym I was constantly booked. The consensus was, "He looks like he enjoys doing his job, and the people he is training seem to love him too. I think I will sign up!" People are watching, give them an inspiring show.

Lastly on this subject, always remember that we did not create ourselves. I personally believe in a Creator that made me wonderfully to do a particular thing. Spiritual growth is the cornerstone of true success. The things of this world are temporary. We cannot take anything with us when we leave. While we are here we should be honoring the One that gave us life. Without my Lord and Savior, Yeshua the Messiah (Jesus Christ), I would be a lost soul, never willing to pour out to you through this book.

You may not believe what I believe, and that is OK. A great deal of what I have to offer is not from me, but what I learn from studying Him. I spend more time studying the Bible than any self-help book that I own. If you are believer, never be afraid to display your faith through your work. While we have our own missions and agendas, our "main thing" should be in line with that which we were created to do. Never forsake your personal time with God because God will not leave nor forsake you.

Respect: Given & Earned

It is said that respect is not given, but earned. And while that is partially true, it does not tell the entire story. In most cases earning respect is a matter of giving it. Someone earns my respect by being courteous. More importantly, someone earns my respect by giving me time. When people give you their time, do not waste it. Add value with every conversation.

People that value time discuss ideas. People that do not value your time will talk about Tom, Dick, Harry, and Joe. We should want people to be excited about our conversations. If you begin to notice that people do not want to spend time with you, take a look at yourself and examine if you are respecting the time that you are spending with them and adding value to relationship.

Rest & Relaxation

Rest and Relaxation are not to be ignored. Throughout this entire book I have been speaking about achieving your goals. What good is it to win if you cannot celebrate your victory? Schedule time to do the things you enjoy. Take a break and rejuvenate. Ambitious Go Getters like us can easily get caught up in our work because we are passionate about it. Spend time doing other things you love with the people you love. At the end of it all, we work so we can have more time to relax.

In the Bible's account of creation, God worked for six days and rested on the seventh. You will receive your healing on the days you take it easy. You need these day sevens to be able to face the stresses of days one through six. So set aside time to enjoy your hobbies. Invest in your family, in your spouse, your children, parents, and siblings. You deserve it. What is success without the people you love?

Rest and Relaxation will increase your productivity. You will be able to work harder and get more accomplished because you will have more energy. In fitness if you want to improve your performance drastically you can do High Intensity Interval Training (HIIT). HIIT is a method of working hard for a short amount of time and resting for even shorter time before hitting it hard again. HIIT training is known to improve your cardiovascular health while preserving your muscle mass. Think of Olympic sprinters. A sprinter is likely to be more muscular than a marathoner. Incorporating short rests into your life will help you attack life with the same type of intensity that Usain Bolt attacks the track.

Epilogue

Success is a relative term. Subjective in nature, success can be whatever we want it to be. For some, success is millions of dollars. For others, it is a championship. Success to me is fulfilling the purpose ordained for my life. The truth is, we are all successful at something. Yet, there are many things we still would like to accomplish. This book was intended to help you discover your path. Success cannot be determined if it lacks purpose. I hope this writing sparked a strong desire inside of you to become more passionate about discovering your purpose and passionately pursue it.

When I was kid, success was more of a photograph than a portrait. My idea of success was a big house, a big necklace, a gold and platinum rollie (Rolex watch) with baguettes, cash to burn, and the baddest women you ever seen! I had a dope boy outlook. I had been corrupted by the desire of fast money and fast living at an early age. I Desired to be rich without an understanding of what it was to be wealthy. That was the image I had of success when I was growing up. Everyone that had jobs seemed to be struggling, but my uncle who sold drugs and pimped gave me hundred dollar bills for making my bed or running to the store. Then there were the athletes and celebrities whose lifestyles mirrored the drug dealers. A person without purpose would easily fall victim to chasing this ideology of success. I did and it almost cost me my life on more than one occasion.

Success to me as an "enlightened" adult looks a lot different. My viewpoint likely shifted when I was homeless and had lost everything. During that time I was able to reflect on life more deeply than usual. In that timeframe I learned to be content with me and realized that despite my situation, I was still OK. I had shelter every day, even though some days it was in my car. I ate every day, even though it may have been some days with only one meal, it was meal. And I never had to beg for help because inherently I always had a hustler's mentality. The most important thing I learned during this time was the power of God. It was during this stage of my life that I was face to face with God and came to the knowledge and truth of Him. Success from this stage of life would take on a new array of colors. Before, success was "what I could get out of life." Success has since become "what can I give life." Success is now more of a portrait. A portrait of significance.

The five plays or steps in this book are intended to give you a guide to achieving significance. At the root of our desires lies being significant. That is what we really want. We want to be valuable. The thing is, you are already valuable. Our programming has been manipulated and screwed up. We were taught to think that our job, status, or our possessions are what make us a success, what makes us significant. You were made to be significant. You were made with a purpose. The main objective now is to discover what that is. You can Get "It," whatever "It" may be, if you are *genuine*, devise a plan and *execute* it with *tact*, using your God given *intelligence*, while valuing *time*. You can GET IT and everything you need. You've already GOT IT! And know this, being a Go Getter means being a Go Giver. We reap what we sow.

My old pastor used to tell us not to become constipated believers. In other words, do not spend all of your time learning and none of your time doing. I encourage you to quickly apply what you have taken from this book and be generous in sharing the knowledge with others. If you have success from applying these principles, please share your stories with me at ronslifespeaks@gmail.com.

References

All biographical references unless noted otherwise in text or references:
Wikipedia.com
Biography.com

All quotes unless noted in text or references:
Google.com
CelebrityTypes.com
Brainyquotes.com

Markuss Persson & Minecraft
Forbes The 2015 Billionaires Issue

Stevie Wonder
http://www.freep.com/article/20140810/COL01/308100085/
Margaret-John-Stevie-Wonder-Shared-piano-broken-Detroit-dreams

Golf & Donald Trump:
http://golftips.golfsmith.com/golf-business-world-20691.html
http://golf.about.com/cs/golfterms/g/bldef_approach.htm

50 Cent Profile:

celebritynetworth.com/articles/entertainment-articles/
how-much-did-50-cent-make-off-vitamin-water/

The 50th Law

http://www.feelingsuccess.com/5-life-lessons-from-50-cent/

Steve Jobs:

https://hbr.org/2012/04/the-real-leadership-lessons-of-steve-jobs
http://www.inc.com/jeff-haden/7-inspirational-steve-jobs-quotes-
that-will-change-your-life.html

Personality Types:

16personalities.com
myersbriggs.org
humanmetrics.com

SWOT Analysis:

https://www.mindtools.com/pages/article/newTMC_05_1.htm

Need Help?

I am available for one-on-one coaching. Email me at ron@ronslifespeaks.com with the Subject: "Coaching". I will work with you personally to Discover Your Purpose & Live It with Passion.

Looking for A Speaker?

If you are looking for an engaging speaker that infuses humor and wisdom in every talk… We should talk! I am available for Keynotes, Seminars, & Workshops. Book me at http://ronslifespeaks.com/contact.

Join My Mailing List!

GET FREE STUFF… Learn about upcoming events, projects, and if you need it, the occasional swift kick in the butt!

Make a Difference!

Help me Mentor 10,000 Kids!!! Watch this video: http://huddleupkids.com and if you like what you see… SHARE IT!

www.ingramcontent.com/pod-product-compliance
Lightning Source LLC
La Vergne TN
LVHW051126080426
835510LV00018B/2250